get MESSY!

We are grateful for funding received from the Church of England's FLOURISH initiative, enabling partnerships between schools and their local churches, aiming to engage a large number of children, young people, and their families in worshipping communities based in schools.

BRF Ministries

15 The Chambers, Vineyard, Abingdon OX13 3FE
+44 (0)1865 319700 | brf.org.uk

The **Messy Church®** name and logo are registered trade marks of Bible Reading Fellowship, a charity (233280) and company limited by guarantee (301324), registered in England and Wales

EU Authorised Representative: Easy Access System Europe – Mustamäe tee 50, 10621 Tallinn, Estonia, **gpsr.requests@easproject.com**

ISBN 978 1 80039 333 2

First published 2025

All rights reserved

This edition © Bible Reading Fellowship 2025

Acknowledgements

Scripture quotations marked with the following abbreviations are taken from the version shown. NCV: the New Century Version®. Copyright © 2005 by Thomas Nelson. Used by permission. All rights reserved. ICB: The Holy Bible, International Children's Bible® Copyright© 1986, 1988, 1999, 2015 by Tommy Nelson™, a division of Thomas Nelson. Used by permission. MSG: *The Message*, copyright © 1993, 1994, 1995, 1996, 2000, 2001, 2002 by Eugene H. Peterson. Used by permission of NavPress. All rights reserved. Represented by Tyndale House Publishers, Inc. NIV: The Holy Bible, New International Version®, NIV® Copyright © 1973, 1978, 1984, 2011 by Biblica, Inc.® Used by permission. All rights reserved worldwide. NLT: The Holy Bible, New Living Translation, copyright © 1996, 2004, 2007, 2013. Used by permission of Tyndale House Publishers, Inc., Carol Stream, Illinois 60188. All rights reserved.

Subeditor: Becca Turnbull

Designer: Ben Bloxham

Proofreader: Daniele Och

Cover photos: © BRF Ministries

Internal photos: © BRF Ministries. Activity photos © session writers.

Photocopying for churches

To order back issues of *Get Messy!* and other Messy Church resources, email BRF Ministries at **enquiries@brf.org.uk** or telephone **+44 (0)1865 319700**.

Send in news, stories, photos and general enquiries to our Messy Church administrator on **+44 (0)1235 858238** or **messychurch@brf.org.uk**.

What is Messy Church?

It's **church**, but not as you know it.

Every month thousands of people of all ages come together to discover Jesus, including those who've never been to church before. In over 30 countries around the world, we eat, play and worship together. Expect activities, songs and prayers and an entirely new way to express your faith.

———

Look out for the following symbols by activities, which give you extra materials and more!

SUPPORT MATERIAL
This symbol means you can go to **messychurch.org.uk/getmessyvol3-3332** to download templates at A4 size, including a session planning sheet.

MESSY CHURCH AT HOME
Activities with this symbol can be used for 'take-home' ideas, to continue the God-conversation between Messy Church gatherings.

MESSY CHURCH GOES WILD
This symbol shows activities that work well for Messy Church Goes Wild sessions. See **messychurch.org.uk/goeswild** for more ideas.

contents

07   **AIKE WRITES**

09   **SEPTEMBER**
HOPE: PUTTING YOUR TRUST IN GOD

14   **OCTOBER**
COMPASSION: 'BEING KIND TO ALL PEOPLE'

21   **NOVEMBER**
PEACE: HOW CAN I BE A PEACEMAKER?

26   **DECEMBER**
JOY: TO THE WHOLE WORLD!

31   **JANUARY**
PERSEVERANCE: FOLLOWING JESUS
TAKES PRACTICE

37   **FEBRUARY**
LOVE: HOW DOES THIS GROW?

42   **MARCH**
INTEGRITY: STAND UP AND BE COUNTED

47   **APRIL**
COURAGE: TO FOLLOW JESUS

52   **MAY**
COMMUNITY: A HOME FOR ALL

57   **JUNE**
PURPOSE: WHAT AM I TO DO?

62   **JULY**
JUSTICE

67   **AUGUST**
PATIENCE: WAIT FOR IT!

Meet our session *Writers*

Mary Judkins

Mary Judkins is a member of our volunteer support team and has been involved in volunteer lay ministry since she was a teenager. She leads a Messy Church Goes Wild in Cornwall and is passionate about children, young people and families meeting Jesus and becoming disciples.

Trish Hahn

Trish Hahn loves to spend time walking on the seafront with her dog Pip. With three children, four carers and a vicar husband, life at the Manse is generally chaotic and very busy. Trish is also the youth pastor at their local church and the Messy Church SEND advisor.

Johannah Myers

Johannah Myers is the associate director of Messy Church USA and, since 2013, has led a Messy Church at the church where she works as the director of disciple formation. She has a passion for intergenerational faith formation and all things Messy.

Anna Lloyd

Anna Lloyd is head of church and community engagement at Street Child and is married to the Revd Dr Dave Lloyd, founding trustee of Street Child. They live in Norfolk with two fantastic teenage kids and together facilitate a network of missional community churches called Garden Church.

Julian Mayer

Julian Mayer is over the moon to be contributing to this edition of Get Messy! Over the past seven years, her love of Messy Church has continued to grow after witnessing firsthand the impact it has had on her church. She currently serves as the director of Christian education and faith formation at St Paul United Church of Christ in Waterloo, Illinois.

Ximena Wilson

Ximena Wilson is fundraising manager for churches, schools and community at Street Child. She is passionate about creating educational resources that inspire and empower the younger generation to make a difference in the lives of their peers in some of the world's toughest places.

Greg Ross

Greg Ross is a Uniting Church Minister and is one of the regional coordinators for Messy Church Western Australia. He is passionate about building up local congregations to collaborate with God on mission in each community, so everyone is welcome at church.

Helen Laird

Helen Laird is the children's and youth development officer for the West Midlands United Reformed Church Synod, and has been involved with Messy Church for over 20 years. She is passionate about enabling faith journeys to happen across all ages. Helen loves to read, and loves all sorts of craft activities.

Becky May

Becky May is founder of The Resources Cupboard, supporting the local church to make young disciples. She helps lead a Messy Church and enjoys engaging with Messy Church with her family. Becky is a member of the Messy Church writing and training teams.

Anne Offler

Anne Offler is based in County Durham and has worked with Sharon Pritchard and numerous Messy Churches for many years. Anne is a Methodist local preacher and writes resources for churches and children's ministry publications.

Martyn Payne

Formerly part of the Messy Church team at BRF Ministries, *Martyn Payne* has a background in teaching, Bible storytelling and leading all-age worship. He is pastor of a church in Essex, and is part of the gold prayer team.

Sharon Pritchard

Sharon Pritchard lives in County Durham with her husband Alan. She works for the diocese of Durham as the foundational training enabler, training leaders full time. She collects nativities and is a frequent visitor to the Emerald Isle.

Dawn Savidge

Dawn Savidge is passionate about families ministry and runs a project called ParentFuel, which helps support parents grow faith in their family. She also works for an estate ministry project, working with families in need. She has been involved with Messy Church since 2015. She loves the way that it includes the whole family.

Growing Christian Values

An all-age resource exploring how to follow Jesus in everyday life

Growing Christian Values complements the session material in *Get Messy! Volume 3*, so that the same topic can be explored between Messy Church gatherings but using different Bible passages, or it can be used on its own. Written in partnership with Parenting for Faith, *Growing Christian Values* is a discipleship resource comprising twelve sessions that help people of all ages and stages of faith to explore values of hope, peace, generosity, perseverance, love, integrity, courage, purpose, community, justice and patience, that underpin a Christian way of life. It works well for family devotional time or any intergenerational group. Available as separate sessions or the full course.

PDF Download | £1.99 per session
£9.99 for 12 sessions | brfonline.org.uk

D♥nate to
Messy Church

BRF Ministries fundraising team

Our vital ministry supporting Messy Churches across the UK and the world would not be possible without your generous support. Through your donations we are able to offer training, resources, events and more to Messy Churches and their teams, helping people of all ages to encounter Jesus.

Making a donation to Messy Church really does make a huge difference. We are grateful to everyone who has made a donation and to all those who have signed up to become a Friend of Messy Church by making a regular donation of £3 a month or more. These donations make a lasting difference to our work, allowing us to plan for the future.

If you or your church would like to become a Friend of Messy Church, you can do so at **brf.org.uk/friends**.

You can also regularly raise money at no extra cost to yourself by using Give as you Live when you shop online or in some shops. Each purchase you make raises funds which go towards supporting and resourcing Messy Churches. You can find out more and sign up at **brf.org.uk/easy-ways-to-support-brf-at-no-cost-to-you**.

If you would like to make a difference to Messy Church by sponsoring a specific project, please do contact our fundraising team via **giving@brf.org.uk** or call us on **01235 462305**.

*Not all mobile phone networks support text giving. If yours doesn't, your message won't be delivered, and you won't be charged. You can always donate online at **brf.org.uk/donate**. Our privacy policy is available at **brf.org.uk/privacy**.

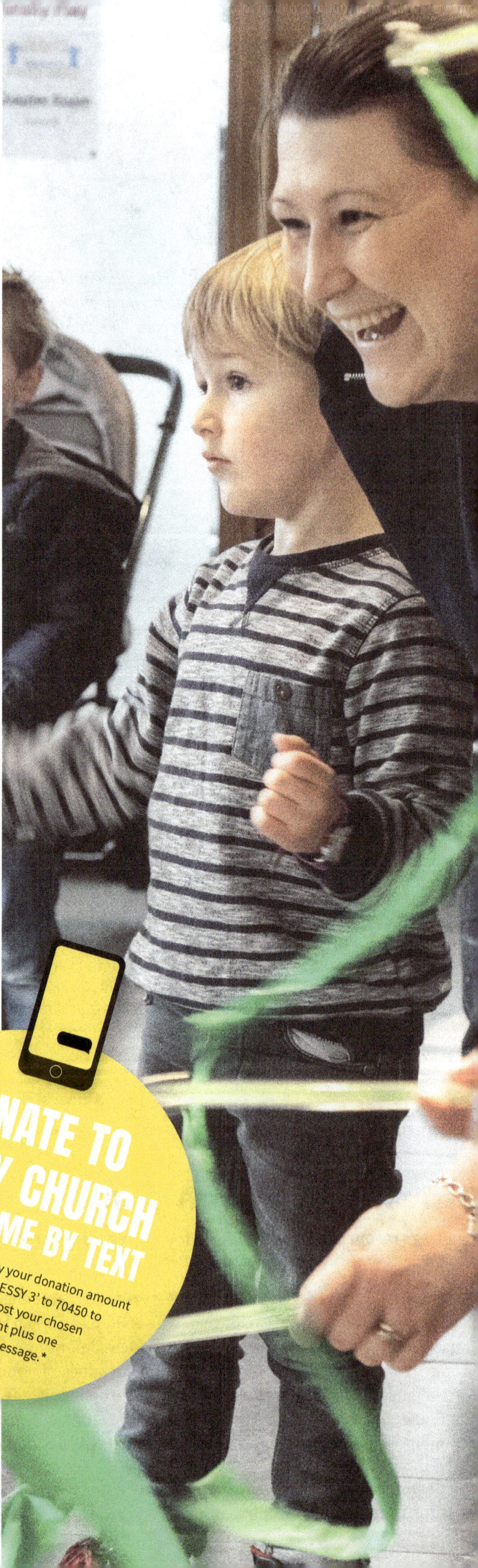

Aike writes...

Welcome to Get Messy! Volume 3

This resource contains twelve session outlines for Messy Churches. We are delighted to work in partnership with FLOURISH, the Church of England initiative to plant new worshipping communities in schools. This volume takes a thematic approach, looking at Christian values and way of life, often covered by school Collective Worship in the UK, enabling Messy Churches that meet in schools to cover the same topic, but with the entire family.

With themes of hope, compassion, peace, perseverance, love, integrity, purpose, justice and patience, Messy Churches can explore values that underpin a Christian way of life. This is the perfect follow-on matierial to *Get Messy! Volume 2: Christian basics made messy*.

The material also includes the key Christian festivals through the lens of the following values: Christmas – joy; Easter – courage; and Pentecost – community.

If you work in a school setting and are looking for Collective Worship material, we recommend the BRF Resource Hub, a one-stop shop for free tried-and-tested ideas from over 20 years of working in primary RE (Barnabas in Schools). To help save time, we've created a webpage at messychurch.brf.org. uk/flourlsh/brf-resource-hub-get-messy-toplcs llstlng Collective Worship and classroom ideas that complement each *Get Messy! Volume 3* session.

As part of the FLOURISH initiative, iSingPOP, Out of the Ark Music and Nick and Becky Drake (Worship for Everyone) have provided song suggestions for each session. Out of the Ark Music have even created a webpage (outoftheark.com/ messychurch), kindly gifting us their song suggestions all in one place. We hope all ages enjoy learning new worship songs together. You can find out a little about each music group on the next page.

We have a special treat in store for January's 2026 session on 'perseverance'. Our Australian Messy friends have worked in partnership with Andrew McDonough, creator of 'Cecil the lost sheep'. Andrew has created a webpage, accessible via a QR code, so that Messy Churches can download PowerPoint slides of his story to use during the celebration – amazing!

How to use Get Messy!

Other than the key Christian festivals: Christmas, Easter and Pentecost, the sessions are standalone, so can be done in any order. Feel free to choose topics that are most suitable for your context.

Remember that any resource is a springboard for you to creatively adapt ideas for your Messy Church. If the themes in this edition are not the right fit, we have a massive back catalogue of resources available on the Messy Church website (messychurch.brf.org.uk/resources/ messy-church-sessions-themes).

We suggest you start your planning meeting by praying and reflecting on where you noticed God at work in your previous session. Perhaps there were 'God conversations' that might need following up? Then read the Bible together and be curious about which words or verses stand out. This will help your team talk about the key Bible themes that you wish to share during the activity time and provides you with a fantastic opportunity for team discipleship. You'll find a choice of ten activities, designed for a range of ages, abilities and spiritual styles, with both indoor and Messy Church Goes Wild (outdoor) suggestions. Remember you don't have to do them all! As we continue to work towards more eco-friendly activities, try to reduce your waste, reuse what you already have in the back of your church cupboard and think about how any craft items can be recycled after Messy Church.

In the 'Add value' section, we've included discussion starter mealtime cards, designed to keep the conversation flowing when you gather to eat. The social action idea can help your Messy Church be church throughout the month. In the 'Celebration' section you'll find ideas to retell the Bible story in an engaging way, together with a prayer, plus song and meal suggestions.

Huge thanks go to our writers who have taken time to create and test-drive these sessions, especially those who are writing for the first time.

If you want to keep up to date with Messy Church news, blogs and training events, sign-up to our monthly enewsletter (messychurch.brf.org.uk/newsletter) and follow us on social media.

Visit messychurch.org.uk/ getmessyvol3–3332 to download all sorts of extra content for these sessions, including support material, photos, table signs, mealtime cards and a planning template!

Out of the Ark Music

Out of the Ark Music was born out of a passionate belief that children deserve the very best. Good songs leave a lasting impression and contain huge potential to make a difference to our lives. The importance of music and the arts cannot be emphasised enough and, though often overlooked, they are a vital part of our children's education. Our goal is…

- To enhance and expand children's enjoyment of music and the world around them by producing songs that are thought provoking, relevant and most of all great fun to sing.
- To produce top-quality materials to give today's children music which excites them and to which they can readily relate.
- To teach about music using traditional methods i.e. by providing strong melodies, interesting song structures and clever rhymes and combining these with modern musical arrangements.
- To preserve the best of our musical and literary heritage whilst embracing modern styles and instrumentation.
- To write good positive songs that re-enforce self-worth and significance and that are appropriate to children's experience.
- To convey truth and teach about Christian values and faith.
- To make all our resources completely teacher-friendly and to support our customers through excellent customer service.

Visit **outoftheark.com/messychurch** to find songs that match the themes in *Get Messy! Volume 3*.

Our mission is to empower children, parents, schools, churches and communities to find their voice, and know they are loved. We support schools in creating inspirational collective worship and equip churches with the confidence to reach out to the intergenerational church.

Worship for Everyone is a Christian faith-based movement to resource and equip collective singing in churches, schools and families. Worship for Everyone seeks to be not purely 'family worship' but 'family-of-God worship' – elevating the importance of children while engaging every age and stage of life. Worship for Everyone seeks to demonstrate and release the power of unity across generations in worship, believing in the intergenerational formation that comes from worshipping as the big family of God.

Session material: September
Hope: putting your trust in God
by Trish Hahn

 **SUPPORT MATERIAL**    **MESSY CHURCH AT HOME**    **MESSY CHURCH GOES WILD**

Bible story for prep

Jeremiah 29:1–14 (NCV)

This is the letter that Jeremiah the prophet sent from Jerusalem to the elders who were among the captives, the priests, and the prophets. He sent it to all the other people Nebuchadnezzar had taken as captives from Jerusalem to Babylon. (This letter was sent after all these people were taken away: Jehoiachin the king and the queen mother; the officers and leaders of Judah and Jerusalem; and the craftsmen and metalworkers from Jerusalem.) Zedekiah king of Judah sent Elasah son of Shaphan and Gemariah son of Hilkiah to Babylon to Nebuchadnezzar king of Babylon. So Jeremiah gave them this letter to carry to Babylon:

This is what the Lord All-Powerful, the God of Israel, says to all those people I sent away from Jerusalem as captives to Babylon: 'Build houses and settle in the land. Plant gardens and eat the food they grow. Get married and have sons and daughters. Find wives for your sons, and let your daughters be married so they also may have sons and daughters. Have many children in Babylon; don't become fewer in number. Also do good things for the city where I sent you as captives. Pray to the Lord for the city where you are living, because if good things happen in the city, good things will happen to you also.' The Lord All-Powerful, the God of Israel, says: 'Don't let the prophets among you and the people who do magic fool you. Don't listen to their dreams. They are prophesying lies to you, saying that their message is from me. But I did not send them,' says the Lord.

This is what the Lord says: 'Babylon will be powerful for seventy years. After that time I will come to you, and I will keep my promise to bring you back to Jerusalem. I say this because I know what I am planning for you,' says the Lord. 'I have good plans for you, not plans to hurt you. I will give you hope and a good future. Then you will call my name. You will come to me and pray to me, and I will listen to you. You will search for me. And when you search for me with all your heart, you will find me! I will let you find me,' says the Lord. 'And I will bring you back from your captivity. I forced you to leave this place, but I will gather you from all the nations, from the places I have sent you as captives,' says the Lord. 'And I will bring you back to this place.'

Pointers

- The nation of Judah turned away from God and sought protection from pagan nations (Assyrians, Egyptians and Babylonians). God's people were in exile in Babylon after Nebuchadnezzar (king of Babylon) had captured Jerusalem.
- The people of Judah were in desperate need of guidance from God as they lived in exile.
- God chose the prophet Jeremiah to deliver God's message.
- Jeremiah's message was challenging and not well received by most people.
- Jeremiah urged the people to return and seek God with all their heart and obey God's commands.
- God revealed through Jeremiah that God had a plan and purpose for the prosperity of God's people, even when their situation was looking hopeless.

How does this session help people grow in Christ?

This session helps people realise that God has a plan and purpose for each of us. Regardless of our current situation, God can work through it to give us hope. We can rely on God if we build a personal relationship with God, encouraged by being part of a Christ-centred community, especially during tough times. God says when we search for God with all our heart, we will find God (vv. 12–14).

Add value

Mealtime card

- What challenges did the people of Judah face that led them to turn away from God?
- What challenges do you face?
- Have you ever felt like giving up on a task that God has asked you to do? What might encourage you?

Question to start and end the session

So… are you willing to trust and place all your confidence and hope in God?

Social action idea

The Faith in Action project encourages students to actively consider the call to follow Jesus in all aspects of life. Encourage young people to activate their faith by advocating for social justice and helping those in need. How could your young people engage in a social activity within their community?

Activities

1. Marble maze game

You will need: Lego pieces in different colours; a square Lego board; marbles

Build a tall maze using Lego pieces and leave gaps for the marble to roll through. Tilt and twist your maze to move the marble until you reach the centre. Time yourself or a friend to see how quickly you can complete the marble maze.

Talk about how easy or hard it was to keep the marble on your planned course. What different materials could you use instead of Lego to make the marble maze faster or slower? Sometimes life is a bit like wandering around a maze – we don't always know which way to go, we come across a dead end and we can feel like we're back at the beginning! When we pray and listen to God, sometimes God gives us insight into the direction to go in. We can test this out with trusted friends who may have more experience of listening to God and walking in God's ways.

I wonder… have you ever felt God has given you a specific direction or task to do? Share your story. What direction in life might God have for you?

2. Ball maze sensory bag

You will need: A4 white paper; a black permanent marker; marble; large sealable bag; clear hand gel or hair gel; clear Sellotape

Using a permanent marker, draw a maze on A4 paper and tape it to a flat surface or tabletop. Fill a sealable bag with clear hand or hair gel and add a small marble. Seal the bag and place it over the maze.

Talk about what fun things you can use to help roll the marble along the maze. Have you ever walked through a maze? Could you find the centre or did you get lost? What helps us find our way out of a maze?

I wonder… if life were a maze, where would you be on your journey? At the start? Lost? In a dead end? Or with a clear sense of direction?

3. Race against the clock

You will need: a white paper plate; tiny pompoms; paper straws; sand timer; a permanent marker

Use a permanent marker or a printed picture to create a more complex maze, which you then stick on to the white paper plate. Use a tiny pompom and straw to blow the pompom around the maze, trying to avoid going outside the lines. Race against your friends to complete the maze against the clock.

Talk about what helped and what made it harder to keep the pompom on track. Life can sometimes feel like a competitive race and it can be challenging to follow the path you want to stay on. Trusting God every step of the way will help strengthen your faith. Share a time when you've had to rely on God or others, when you might have otherwise been blown off course?

I wonder... how can this game teach us more about patience and staying 'on track' in life? What helps us and what gets in the way of us trusting God?

4. Hope letter 

You will need: writing paper; an envelope; pens or pencils

In a quiet space, write a letter to God saying how you're currently feeling, maybe retelling what you've been through this past month, what's on your mind and what your hopes and dreams are for the next six months.

Take a moment to pause, invite the Holy Spirit to guide your thoughts and then write a letter to yourself from God in response. What does God want to say to you?

Younger people could draw emojis or a picture of how they feel right now and how they would like to feel in the future.

Put your letter and response from God in an envelope, addressed to yourself. You might like to stick a stamp on it. Ask a trusted friend or your Messy Church leader to send it to you in six months' time, when you might need to read some hope-filled messages.

Talk about the different ways you can search and listen for God's direction – through the Bible, nature, audible voice, a thought in your head, through discerning Christian friends. Share a personal example of when God has guided you.

I wonder... what does it mean to seek God with all your heart?

5. Babylonian banquet blind taste test

You will need: blindfolds; small plates/ bowls/cups; a selection of food/drink from the Middle East (such as figs, vinegar, honey, milk, watermelon, pumpkin, yoghurt, grapes, barley bread, olive oil, water)

Remember to risk assess for allergies and intolerances. Place each food item in a small plate or bowl or in a cup. Using a blindfold, ask volunteers to taste and smell a different food item and guess what it is.

Talk about what foods you have for breakfast. Compare this to what the captives in Babylon might have eaten in the taste test. What type of food do you like best? Jeremiah's message to the captives was to plant gardens and eat the food they grew, as they would be living in Babylon for 70 years before God would rescue them. Could you wait 70 years to eat your favourite food again?

I wonder... are you good at trying new foods when you go to new places? Is God asking you to try something new in the season ahead?

6. What's in the bag?

You will need: a cotton or cloth bag; a pinecone; a small bouncy ball; a squishy toy; a glove; crinkly material; a glove puppet; dry pasta; a toy car

Places the various objects into the bag. Take it in turns to place your hand inside the cloth bag and feel the shape of the items inside, trying to guess what they might be.

Talk about if you were hesitant to touch an item. Were there moments when you were worried? When something is unknown/unseen, we can hesitate and feel frightened. In the Bible, Jeremiah had a message for God's people, giving them direction in an unfamiliar and anxious place.

I wonder... are you facing an unfamiliar situation? Are you anxious or excited about what's ahead?

7. Obstacle course

You will need: a variety of significant obstacles placed around a garden or hall; blindfolds

Work in pairs, with one person blindfolded. The blindfolded person must navigate past various obstacles placed around the space, following a twisty and winding path, only listening to the verbal commands from their partner. When you've finished, swap roles so everyone gets a go.

Talk about what it was like being blindfolded. Did your partner give good instructions? Were you able to trust their directions – why or why not?

I wonder… who do you trust to help you navigate through life's big and little decisions? What does it look like to trust God to guide us?

8. What might Jeremiah look like?

You will need: twigs; pinecones; stones; wild grass; charcoal; moss; pieces of wood; bark; soil

Unleash your creativity and dive into nature! Gather a variety of natural materials and craft your very own unique Jeremiah. Let your imagination run wild and create something quite extraordinary!

Talk about the different materials you could use to create the expression you would like his face to show. Would he look fierce or calm?

I wonder… what do you think about Jeremiah's message from God?

9. I know you have a plan for me, O Lord

You will need: A4 coloured paper; coloured pens; scissors; ribbon; sticky glue dots

Make a heart out of the materials available. Write or draw a prayer or poem on it to support those who are feeling hopeless or those who are doubting and struggling to trust God with their future direction. This could be a prayer for yourself!

Talk about how reading the Bible can help us to understand God's plan for our lives. We can trust God to take care of our hearts. Share a story of what happened when you trusted God in a situation.

I wonder… what do you think God's plan for your future will be?

10. How can we help those in need?

You will need: up-to-date information on food banks in and around your local area

Local food banks depend on volunteers to offer emergency food and practical support to individuals facing difficult times and loss of direction.

Talk about how many individuals face the uncertain challenge of making ends meet, often struggling with the harsh reality of securing money for essentials like food, clothing and utilities. It can be a constant worry for some people and people can lose hope.

I wonder… in what creative ways can you contribute to your local food bank and practically show God's love and hope to those who are facing challenges?

Celebration

*Demonstrate the BSL Christian sign for hope (**christianbsl. com/vocabulary/hope**). Rather than just crossing our fingers for 'wishful thinking' (the lottery symbol), as we do the Christian BSL sign, we move our hand over our heart and make a fist, like we're grabbing on to something more certain – the hope we have in Christ!*

You will need two volunteers. One will wear a blindfold and the other will shine a bright torch. You will also need a large map. The person wearing the blindfold will hold the map but cannot see it. The person holding the torch can shine the light on to the map to see which direction to go.

Narrator Today's story is about giving hope. This Bible story happened over 2,500 years ago. It offers hope for the future of the nation of Judah during a time of uncertainty and doubt among its people, when they were being held captive in Babylon. Jeremiah the prophet sent the captives a letter with this message.

Jeremiah I have a very important message from God, so open your ears, all people of Judah.

A small crowd of people talking among themselves, looking uncertain and worried, turn and listen to Jeremiah as he speaks.

Jeremiah God has detailed plans for all of you. God plans to give you good things and a bright future, and God will help you through the tough times in your life and give you hope. God wants you all to be his special friends. God wants to talk to you and to listen to your prayers. It's like you've all been walking around blindfolded. (The *blindfolded person tries to walk forward but bumps into a chair.*) You can't see what Is before you, so you stop moving and stand still. Take a moment to listen to God's voice. (The *small crowd stand up and cup their hand to their ear to listen to Jeremiah speaking.*) God wants you to follow God's best path in life. Look inside your heart and find God waiting for you.

The person with the torch takes hold of the map and verbally directs the blindfolded person to move forward, avoiding obstacles, until they are standing in front of Jeremiah.

Narrator God is a bit like the person with the torch, giving instructions to find your way on the map. If you are listening well, you will realise that God has been guiding you all along. (*Person removes blindfold and shakes hands with the person who has guided them.*) Trust in the Lord your God, who plans to give you a hope and a future.

I wonder...

- What plans do I hope for?
- What is God's special purpose for me?
- How can I serve God today?

Prayer

Thank you, God of hope, that you have a plan for each one of us and that you will give us hope and a bright future. Help us trust you completely, even when we cannot see the path before us. Help us put our plans into your hands and allow you to guide us forward. Amen.

Song suggestions

- 'Jeremiah 29:11 – For I know the plans I have for you' – Calm Children Collection
- 'Jeremiah 29:11 – Memory verse song' – Hillsong Kids
- 'Jeremiah 29:11 – Hope and a future' – Seeds Family Worship
- 'All over the world' – iSingPOP
- 'Benediction song' – Ark Music Collective
- 'Hope' – Nick and Becky Drake (Worship for Everyone)

Meal suggestions

Chicken soup with barley bread. Follow it up with a healthy fruit salad. You might want to include a selection of fruits, dates, watermelon and grapes and then serve with honey and vanilla ice cream.

Session material: October

Compassion: 'being kind to all people'

by Anna Lloyd and Ximena Wilson from Street Child

Bible story for prep

Leviticus 19:9–10 (ICB)

'You harvest your crops on your land. But do not harvest all the way to the corners of your fields. If grain falls onto the ground, don't gather it up. Don't pick all the grapes in your vineyards. And don't pick up the grapes that fall to the ground. You must leave those things for poor people. You must also leave them for people travelling through your country. I am the Lord your God.'

Ruth 2:1–9

Now there was a rich man living in Bethlehem whose name was Boaz. Boaz was one of Naomi's close relatives from Elimelech's family.

One day Ruth, the woman from Moab, said to Naomi, 'Let me go to the fields. Maybe someone will be kind and let me gather the grain he leaves in his field.'

Naomi said, 'Go, my daughter.'

So Ruth went to the fields. She followed the workers who were cutting the grain. And she gathered the grain that they had left. It just so happened that the field belonged to Boaz. He was a close relative from Elimelech's family.

When Boaz came from Bethlehem, he spoke to his workers: 'The Lord be with you!'

And the workers answered, 'May the Lord bless you!'

Then Boaz spoke to his servant who was in charge of the workers. He asked, 'Whose girl is that?'

The servant answered, 'She is the Moabite woman who came with Naomi from the country of Moab. She said, "Please let me follow the workers and gather the grain that they leave on the ground." She came and has remained here. From morning until just now, she has stopped only a few moments to rest in the shelter.'

Then Boaz said to Ruth, 'Listen, my daughter. Stay here in my field to gather grain for yourself. Do not go to any other person's field. Continue following behind my women workers. Watch to see which fields they go to and follow them. I have warned the young men not to bother you. When you are thirsty, you may go and drink. Take water from the water jugs that the servants have filled.'

Pointers

- In Leviticus 19:9–10, God is telling us not to be greedy. God is saying we should give our extra resources, money and food to people who need them. We read a similar message in the story of Ruth. Have a read of Ruth 2.

- The passage in Leviticus and the story of Ruth reveal God's heart and intention for us to be generous and kind, to share the excess of our 'harvest' with those who are in need, and to look out for the foreigner and stranger.

- The story of Ruth is a great one to read during the season of Harvest. We see Boaz and his household gleaning and gathering their harvest from the fields and making sure that when they do so they don't hoard it all for themselves but share it with those who are in need – in this case Ruth. Ruth is not only given the spare grain, but she is also given shelter where she can rest (Ruth 2:7, 12), water (Ruth 2:9), kindness (Ruth 2:10) and food (Ruth 2:14).

- The compassion shown to Ruth gives her hope and safety during a very difficult time in her life. She is a foreigner in a strange land, a long way away from her home. She is a widow, having lost her husband unexpectedly, and she is in need financially.

- The work of the charity Street Child is a modern example of people working together to help the world's most vulnerable children. Street Child works in over 25 countries to help those who have been affected by war, natural disasters and poverty. It provides safe spaces for children to play and be given the care they need. Like Boaz, Street Child helps people in the toughest of circumstances, providing shelter, kindness, vital resources and education.

How does this session help people grow in Christ?

This session will help people explore the importance of giving from our excess. The session will explore themes of sharing, kindness, compassion, generosity and social action as modelled by Boaz in Ruth 2, and it will introduce the work of the charity Street Child.

Add value

Mealtime card

- What resources do we have plenty of and how can we share them?

- How else can we be generous and kind?

- How can we look out for those who are most vulnerable?

- What could we do to support the work of Street Child?

Question to start and end the session

So… how can we be generous and kind to those in need around us and across the world?

Social action idea

Can you arrange a fundraising event with your friends, family or community to raise money for Street Child so that they can help people in need? This is an opportunity to be creative and proactive. FUNdraising can be FUN!

How about a sponsored football match, bake sale, fashion show or concert? Street Child's colour is orange, so you could have an orange-themed party to help raise awareness. Contact **churches@street-child.org** for stickers, posters, bunting and more. Alternatively, you could discuss and pray about who else you might like to bless with the gift of your fundraising – it could be a local charity.

Activities

1. Build an indoor den/shelter

You will need: large household objects and furniture (e.g. chairs, coffee tables, boxes, clothes airer); blankets; pillows/cushions; rugs; pegs; string; lantern/torch

In the story of Ruth, Ruth rests in a shelter provided by Boaz. As a group, work together to build a shelter using the resources around you. What makes a good shelter? Be creative in making a strong, useable and nice/fun place for someone to rest.

Talk about what would have made Ruth feel safe, comfortable and looked after in the shelter provided by Boaz.

I wonder… what things would make you feel safe if needing to shelter in an emergency? Street Child provides safe places for children to be in a variety of global emergencies (e.g. safe play spaces in refugee camps and school buildings in remote regions).

2. School building with Street Child

You will need: box of Lego/Duplo (alternatively, other construction toys such as wooden bricks, junk modelling); a life-size building brick to use as a prop (optional); messy material to make a life-size brick (e.g. mud or clay mixed with straw/sand/gravel, or use playdough for a less messy version)

Firstly, spend some time (as a group or individually) making a school out of Lego/Duplo – or any alternative construction toys/materials. Design and build a school, classroom and/or playground, incorporating ideas which make a school fun and safe! Once made, show and celebrate each model in the group.

Secondly, putting the Lego models to one side and looking at a real brick, spend some time making an actual life-size brick. Give each person a lump of clay, thick mud or play-dough and mix it with gravel/sand/straw/water to make it the right consistency to mould into shape. Try to mould it into the shape and size of a typical brick. Reflect on how this is a method used by many communities in Street Child's projects in Western Africa to build whole schools.

Talk about how Street Child makes sure that children are safe, in school and learning in remote and hard-to-reach places. For example, in Sierra Leone and Liberia in West Africa, Street Child has helped local communities build over 600 schools using local materials and building methods. This often involves making bricks with materials such as straw and mud.

I wonder… what makes a fun playground? What makes a good classroom? What makes a school safe? Why is it harder to build schools in countries like Liberia and Sierra Leone?

3. Build an outdoor den/shelter 

You will need: materials for structure (e.g. large sticks, branches, wooden planks, wooden crates, etc.); materials for cover (e.g. a tarpaulin, sheets, blankets, cardboard); fixings (e.g. logs, rocks, string, tent pegs); furnishings (e.g. logs, rocks, blankets, a lantern/torch, home comforts)

In the story of Ruth, Ruth rests in a shelter provided by Boaz. As a group, work together to build a shelter outdoors using the resources around you. What makes a good shelter? Be creative in making a strong, useable and nice/fun place for someone to rest, bearing in mind the ground and weather conditions. How do these affect your build?

Talk about what would have made Ruth feel safe, comfortable and looked after in the shelter provided by Boaz?

I wonder… what things would make you feel safe if needing to shelter in an emergency? Street Child provides safe places for children to be in a variety of global emergencies (e.g. safe play spaces in refugee camps and school buildings in remote regions).

4. Friendship bracelets and notes of kindness

You will need: a printed copy of the Street Child friendship card; scissors; a pen; beads; an elastic string

Making a friendship bracelet is a fun and creative activity! This is an opportunity for you to give this gift to a child in one of the world's most challenging places. You will have an opportunity to write a short, kind message and attach the bracelet for our team to send it to one of the places Street Child works. Get ready to make a little child smile across the world!

Start by cutting your elastic string into equal lengths, usually about 36 inches (3 feet) each. Cut six pieces of string in the same length. You can adjust the length depending on the size of the bracelet.

Tie a simple knot at the top of the strands, leaving a few inches at the top as a tail. This will help secure the bracelet later.

Attach the knot to a surface using tape or clip it to a clipboard. Make sure it's tight so the strings don't move while you're working. Separate the six strings into three groups of two strings each, so that you have one group in each hand and one group in the middle.

So, you have the left strand, the middle strand, and the right strand. Cross the right strand over the middle strand, so now the right strand is in the middle. Cross the left strand over the new middle strand (which was the right strand). Now the left strand is in the middle.

Repeat these steps, be as creative as you would like and add some beads as you cross the strings! Finish with a knot at the end, and check that the bracelet is the right size.

Cut out the Street Child friendship card, write a kind message and attach the bracelet to the card. Post this card with the bracelet to the Street Child office and our team will make sure to deliver your gift to a child in need. Use the address below:

Ximena Wilson/Anna Lloyd – Community Fundraising team, 33 Creechurch Lane, London, EC3A 5EB, UNITED KINGDOM

Talk about your friends while you make this bracelet and perhaps consider praying for the child who will receive it. Pray for them to have good friends around them and to receive everything they need to be able to go to school and be safe.

I wonder… how would you feel if you received a gift from someone who doesn't know you?

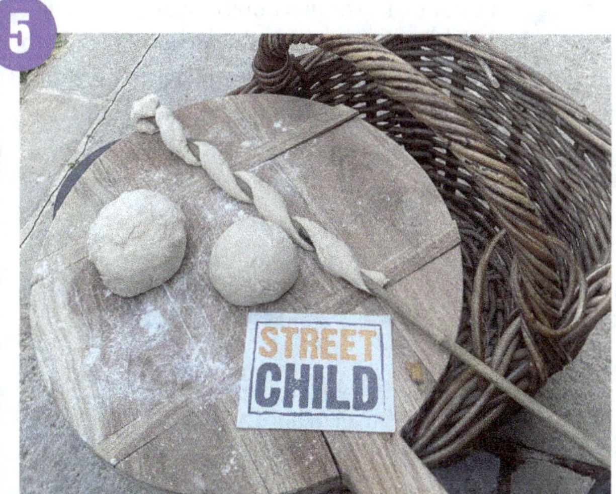

5. Bread-making and baking

You will need: a firepit, pizza oven or normal kitchen oven; sticks, bamboo, skewers to wind the dough on to; balsamic vinegar for dipping; other dipping options (e.g. sugar and cinnamon, honey, melted chocolate, garlic butter, jam); ingredients to make a bread dough (see below); a mixing bowl; a tsp measurer; a sieve; kitchen scales; a jug

Remember to risk assess for allergies and intolerances and risk assess the baking/cooking element, whether that is with a firepit or oven.

This activity will see you making, breaking and sharing bread together, with some tasty extras (we won't be just sticking to Boaz's vinegar dipping option!)

The bread dough recipe is easy to make, but time should be allowed for rising. The dough can either be made from scratch during the Messy Church session (allowing time/a break for the dough to rise) or the dough can be prepared earlier and the activity time used for the shaping and baking of the bread.

Making the dough:
This is enough for five small portions; scale up or down according to number of participants.

- 300 g self-raising flour
- 1 tsp table salt
- 1 tsp yeast
- 2 tsp sugar
- lukewarm water

Instructions:

- Place the flour in a bowl and create a well in the middle.
- Add a teaspoon of yeast to the well and put the sugar on top of the yeast.
- Sprinkle the salt around the edge of the bowl on the flour (not the in the well).
- Add water so that it fills the well.
- Leave for five minutes or until you see small bubbles rising from the water/yeast mixture.
- Mix together with your hands, bringing all the ingredients together.
- Add some more water, little by little so that the mixture forms into a tacky dough
- Knead for five minutes or until the dough is smooth.
- Leave the dough in a bowl, covered by a tea-towel or cling film, in a warm place to rise for one hour.
- Remove the dough from the bowl and knead again, adding a dusting of flour if too sticky.
- Divide into individual portions to be shared out.

Once the dough is ready, provide each person with a share of the batch in the shape of a small ball (5 cm x 5 cm) along with a stick/wooden skewer. An extra dusting of flour might be necessary to stop the dough from sticking. **If baking over a firepit**, the ball should be flattened and hand-rolled into a snake shape – approximately 3 cm wide. This can then be wound around the stick/skewer, securing it to the end point so that it doesn't fall off. **If baking in the oven**, the ball can be hand rolled into a shape and pattern of your choice.

Baking options:
- Firepit baking – if you have access to a firepit outside, then the skewers can be held over the fire and gently turned until the dough is cooked through. Depending on the heat of the fire, this can take 10–20 minutes, but it shouldn't take too long.
- Oven baking – lay the dough shape on a lined and lightly greased baking tray (writing the name of the baker on the baking paper) and bake in a preheated oven (230C/210C fan/gas 8) for 10–15 minutes.

Once baked, dip in tasty dipping options and enjoy eating together!

Talk about how in Ruth 2, Boaz shows kindness not only through his words to Ruth, but also through generous hospitality and sharing a meal with her.

Ruth says in verse 13: 'You are very kind to me, sir. You have said kind words to me, your servant. You have given me hope.' Then Boaz invites Ruth to join him at a mealtime in verse 14: 'Come here! Eat some of our bread. Here, dip your bread in our vinegar.'

Eating together and sharing food meets essential needs of hunger and also builds community and friendship.

I wonder... how can we use food to bless and encourage others? What kind words can you share with those around you who you are eating with?

6. Seeds of kindness  

You will need: collage template/pumpkin outline; a variety of seeds (e.g. pumpkin seeds, bird seeds), lentils, leaves and other autumnal items; glue; scissors

Use seeds, leaves and other autumnal items to decorate the pumpkin template – while thinking about harvest/harvesting. If you have time, you can begin by going outside to look for and gather some natural autumnal objects to include in your collage.

Talk about how in the story of Ruth, Boaz makes sure that spare grain is gathered to give to Ruth. It is roasted and given to her so that she is no longer hungry. At harvest time we think about collecting the fruit, vegetables or grain which have grown from seeds which were planted in a different season. When we see the fruit of these seeds at harvest time, we give thanks to God for we have been given and seek to share this with others.

I wonder... what resources do you have in your life that you can give thanks for and also share?

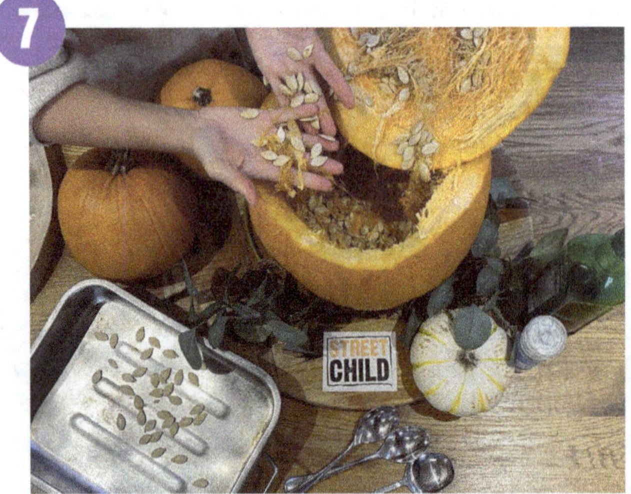

7. Pumpkin seed scooping, counting and roasting 

You will need: some large pumpkins; spoons or scoops; a sharp knife for adults; a chopping board; a sieve/colander; a bowl of cold water; baking trays; olive oil; salt; an oven; a calculator

Remember to risk assess for allergies and using the knife.

This is a messy, fun and interactive activity! Have an adult cut open the pumpkin(s) by slicing off the top quarter. Use your hands and/or the spoons to scoop out all pulp and fibre strands. Pick out all the seeds from the messy pulp and put them into a sieve/colander to rinse with cold water (either under a tap or in a bowl of water). Washing them makes them particularly slimy and fun (or icky!) to run your hands through! Use kitchen roll to dry as much as possible then count out on to a baking tray. Count how many seeds were in your pumpkin and make a note of the number!

Drizzle the seeds with some olive oil, add a pinch of salt, and roast them in a preheated oven (200C/180c fan/gas 6) for 10 minutes.

Talk about how many pumpkin seeds were in your pumpkin. Can you count them all? There are lots of stories and metaphors in the Bible about planting seeds and bringing in the harvest. In verse 6 of 1 Corinthians 3, Paul writes: 'I planted the seed in your hearts, and Apollos watered it, but it was God who made it grow' (NLT). Here Paul is talking about planting seeds of faith. We can all plant seeds of faith, love and kindness in the way we live our lives, interact with those around us and share our resources. It's exciting to think that by planting just one seed, e.g. a pumpkin seed, not only can it grow into a pumpkin, but inside that pumpkin is the potential for hundreds and thousands more pumpkins to grow!

I wonder... what seeds of kindness or generosity can you be planting this week? How might it make a difference and be multiplied?

8. Make a nest with autumn leaves and twigs 

You will need: foraged natural resources, such as sticks, leaves, feathers, dried flowers, dried grasses, foliage

Go for a forage outside to collect twigs, autumn leaves, straw/dried grass, feathers or flowers – anything you can find to make a comfy nest! Bring together your collection of items with things other people have found, and together or individually create a nest using the steps below. You can make a large one together (of any size, even human size!) or a beautifully formed small one.

- Weave together the twigs and firmer objects in a round bowl shape (see picture).
- Weave in the softer materials, such as moss, straw, feathers and leaves.
- Add extra padding and soft materials into the centre and decorate with colourful or beautiful flowers/leaves.

Talk about how in verses 11 and 12 of Ruth 2, Boaz says to Ruth: ' You came to this nation where you did not know anyone… You have come to him [the God of Israel] as a little bird finds shelter under the wings of its mother.' The picture we have here of shelter and safety is that of a bird finding shelter under its mother's wings. How can we help create places of safety, warmth and hospitality for those who are far from home or feeling lonely?

I wonder… can you see any nests in the trees or hedgerows around you? What else does the Bible have to say about the birds of the air? Read Matthew 6:26.

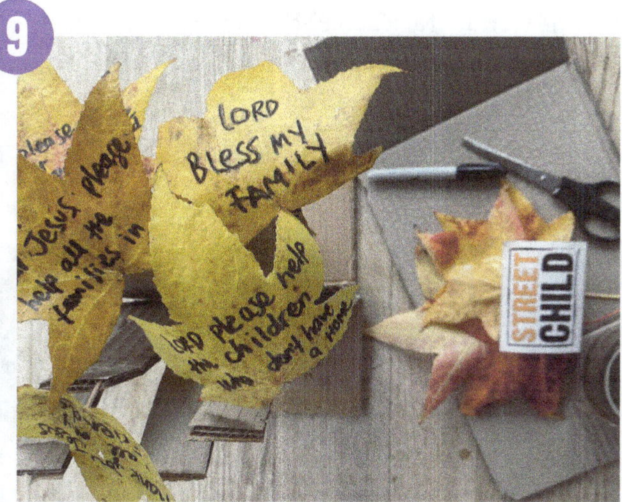

9. Create a prayer tree

You will need: cardboard; tape; a permanent marker; scissors; leaves

Making a prayer tree will encourage you to be very intentional with your prayers! Start by cutting the trunk of the tree and add some roots at the bottom to make it stand. Cut some branches at the top of your tree and bend them slightly to add a branch shape. Secure the trunk and the branches if you need using some tape.

Reflect on the questions below and write what comes to your heart on the leaves using the permanent marker. Write as many prayers as you would like and stick them to your tree using tape.

Talk about what you are thankful for and what are some of the things you love most about God.

I wonder… what are some of the needs you have? What are the needs you think others around you may have? Consider praying for children who have lost everything because of a natural disaster or war. Take some time to pray and maybe write a scripture along with your prayers.

10. Create your own donation jar/tin/bucket

You will need: empty jam jars, buckets or boxes; decorations (tissue paper, crate paper, stickers, ribbons, etc.); PVA glue; scissors; a laptop to watch a film; QR code to print

In the social action segment of this session, we asked you to consider ways to fundraise. In this activity you can make fun collection pots to gather your donations! Make them bright, bold and eye-catching to encourage and inspire people to give to charity and make a difference! Print off and attach the donation QR code too! Watch the video on Street Child's homepage (**street-child.org**) to understand more about the impact of your fundraising and the difference to children's life you can make!

Talk about potential opportunities and events where you could fundraise and raise awareness for Street Child or another local charity.

I wonder… why is it worthwhile taking time to fundraise?

Celebration

Start off with a round-up of the different activities that have been happening in this Messy Church session.

Today's activities have been helping us think about God's heart and call for us to be generous and kind with our resources, and to give to others when we have enough. We have been thinking about building shelters, sharing food and getting creative with the resources God has given us. The story of Ruth and Boaz has helped us think about how we can help others to feel safe, protected, loved and provided for, especially the foreigner or stranger in need.

What words come to mind from the story of Ruth and Boaz? *Kindness, hospitality, generosity, sharing, providing and nurturing are all themes.*

We have also been thinking about how far God's generosity goes and the miracle of multiplication – that by planting a single seed, thousands of apples (or pumpkins!) could grow. *If these activities have been done, hold up the pumpkin pictures and/or pumpkin.*

If God can grow a pumpkin (and thousands more) from a single seed, just imagine how much kindness could grow from you planting just one seed or act of kindness in someone's life!

The work and story of the charity Street Child is a fantastic example of people who are following God's command and call to love our neighbours as ourselves (in this case global neighbours rather than next door neighbours). Street Child's work started 16 years ago as an idea around the kitchen table among a few friends. God took that seed of an idea and helped it grow into a global children's charity which now works in over 25 countries and has helped well over a million children! Street Child helps children who have been affected by terrible circumstances, such as war, natural disasters and poverty. It provides safe spaces for children to play and be given the care they need. It provides education by building schools for children who otherwise are not receiving an education.

What do you think a safe play space or new school might look like for the children affected by war or natural disaster? In Ukraine it has looked like turning dingy basement bomb shelters into colourful fun classrooms, with games and activities, crafts and cosy corners for children to spend their time and be with their friends. In Sierra Leone and Liberia it has looked like building schools in villages and remote areas that have never had a local school before – meaning that children have the chance to learn to read and write for the first time.

Street Child is bringing hope and shining a light in the world for people just like Boaz did for Ruth!

Here is a short video which celebrates and highlights Street Child's reach and impact across lots of different countries around the world: **tinyurl.com/3x3cu6cz**.

I wonder...

- What feelings does this film conjure up in you? Does it make you feel hopeful and excited that you can make a difference to the lives of others by praying and giving?
- What ideas has God given you about being kind and making a difference?

Prayer

Lord, we thank you for all the amazing blessings that you have given us. We are sorry for the times we have forgotten to be grateful for what we have. We ask that as you used Boaz in the story of Ruth to be generous and have compassion, you use us to bless and care for those in need, even when perhaps we don't know them. We know that you do, and you care for them.

Lord, as we reflected on the importance of food, shelter and love, we pray for the families who don't have a home or live in extreme poverty. We pray for your provision for them and your protection.

We pray Psalm 91:1–2 over the people in need around the world: 'Whoever dwells in the shelter of the Most High will rest in the shadow of the Almighty. I will say of the Lord, "He is my refuge and my fortress, my God, in whom I trust"' (NIV).

May all the children and families around the world find refuge and love in you Lord. In Jesus' name. Amen.

Song suggestions

- 'Mighty to save' – Hillsong
- 'Hope on the horizon' – KXC and Rich and Lydia Dicas
- 'God of justice' – Tim Hughes
- 'The blessing' – Kari Jobe
- 'Crying out for love' – Mark and Helen Johnson (Out of the Ark Music)
- 'One world' – Nick and Becky Drake (Worship for Everyone)
- 'This is the day' – iSing POP

Meal suggestions

Make homemade pizzas using some of the bread dough batch used for today's food activity. Alternatively, you can make pizza on pitta bread.

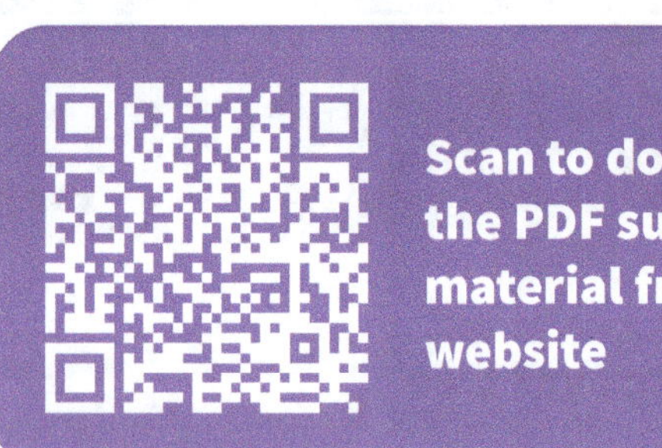

Session material: November
Peace: how can I be a peacemaker?
by Mary Judkins

 **SUPPORT MATERIAL**    **MESSY CHURCH AT HOME**    **MESSY CHURCH GOES WILD**

Bible story for prep

1 Samuel 25:4–34 (MSG, abridged)

David, out in the backcountry, heard that Nabal was shearing his sheep and sent ten of his young men off with these instructions: 'Go to Carmel and approach Nabal. Greet him in my name, "Peace! Life and peace to you. Peace to your household, peace to everyone here!"'… David's young men went and delivered his message word for word to Nabal. Nabal tore into them… David's men got out of there and went back and told David what he had said. David said, 'Strap on your swords!' They all strapped on their swords, David and his men, and set out, four hundred of them… Meanwhile, one of the young shepherds told Abigail, Nabal's wife, what had happened… 'Do something quickly because big trouble is ahead for our master and all of us'… Abigail flew into action. She took two hundred loaves of bread, two skins of wine, five sheep dressed out and ready for cooking, a bushel of roasted grain, a hundred raisin cakes, and two hundred fig cakes, and she had it all loaded on some donkeys. Then she said to her young servants, 'Go ahead and pave the way for me. I'm right behind you'…

As soon as Abigail saw David, she got off her donkey and fell on her knees at his feet, her face to the ground in homage, saying… 'Now take this gift that I, your servant girl, have brought to my master, and give it to the young men who follow in the steps of my master' … And David said, 'Blessed be God, the God of Israel. He sent you to meet me! And blessed be your good sense! Bless you for keeping me from murder and taking charge of looking out for me. A close call! As God lives, the God of Israel who kept me from hurting you, if you had not come as quickly as you did, stopping me in my tracks, by morning there would have been nothing left of Nabal…'

Matthew 5:9 (MSG)

'You're blessed when you can show people how to cooperate instead of compete or fight. That's when you discover who you really are, and your place in God's family.'

Pointers

- Abigail was a peacemaker. Abigail was courageous, generous and humble. Abigail looked after the needs of others.
- God is in charge. Make peace not war – in a world that needs peace, consider our role in conflicts (big and small) and how to diffuse them. Jesus said: 'Blessed are the peacemakers' (Matthew 5:9, NIV).
- Remembrance Day falls in November. Will there ever be peace on earth? How can I be a peacemaker?

How does this session help people grow in Christ?

We can't change overnight! But prayer brings God into the problem and the solution and helps us to take a step back before we act. Our character, our heart and our mind will need to change so we can follow the ultimate peacemaker – Jesus, who gave his life to overcome evil.

In 1 Samuel 25, a beautiful story emerges, one of submission and deliverance. Abigail is a lesser-known heroine in the Bible, a humble woman who was married to a wealthy scoundrel. Abigail combined her wisdom with her wealth to appear before an approaching enemy to plead for the safety of her husband's household.

Without hesitation, and without telling her husband, Abigail gathered together food supplies and loaded them on donkeys. Then she headed out to meet the future king of Israel.

David heeded Abigail's wise words. He respected her for the great respect she showed her husband's household, despite his faulty character. He sent her away with a blessing, promising her safe return home and the preservation of the men of Nabal.

Add value

Mealtime card

- Do you like peace and quiet? Where do you find it?
- What do you think of when you hear the word 'peace'?
- Which do you think is more important – freedom or peace?

Question to start and end the session

So… how can I make peace? How can I keep the peace?

Social action idea

Collect clothes for the homeless and food for the local food bank. Children and young people could also see where they could be kind to someone at school.

Activities

1. Tin can telephone

You will need: empty tin cans (make sure the edges are not sharp); string

Abigail talked to David. How many times have we heard: 'Talk to one another; use kind words not fists'? Take a long length of string (about 150 cm). Make a hole in the can (ask adults to help for safety reasons!) and tie one end of the string to each can.

One person listens and one person talks. Is it easy to hear the other person? Is it easier with a short or long piece of string? try it!

Talk about how because there were no phones when Abigail was alive, she had to go and visit David face to face. What difference did it make actually being with him?

I wonder... do you find it easy or hard to connect with God and share your thoughts with him?

2. 'Expensive' bracelet

You will need: long pipe cleaners; paper straws

Cut the straws into lengths of c. 2 cm. Thread on to a pipe cleaner until it goes around the wrist. Twist to secure.

Talk about how Abigail's husband was rich and so she used her wealth and wisdom to plead for her husband's life. Do you think it's better to be rich or poor? If you don't have much money, how else can you help other people?

I wonder... if God prefers someone to give £1 to help others, or £5, or £50, or £500, or £5,000?

3. A positive out of a negative 

You will need: scraps of wood or wood pieces; small nails; a hammer; wool; a plastic needle with big eyes

Banging nails into the wood can be destructive but can also help you let out anger safely. When you've done a row of five at the top and at the bottom, make a weaving loom with thick thread. Weave assorted colours across it.

Talk about how you feel as you hammer. How did the weaving help? Jesus was nailed to the cross so we could have peace with God. What do you think that means?

I wonder... is it hard to say 'Sorry' when you've been angry with someone? How else can you make peace?

4. World prayer for peace

You will need: copies of the World Council of Churches prayer from 1983 which can be found online (oikoumene.org/resources/documents/prayer-for-peace); pens; pencils

This prayer was written by the World Council of Churches, which brings together churches, denominations and church fellowships in more than 120 countries and territories throughout the world, representing over 580 million Christians and including most of the world's Orthodox churches, scores of Anglican, Baptist, Lutheran, Methodist and Reformed churches, as well as many United and independent churches. Can you illustrate it? Use whatever you like…

Alternatively, can you write a poem about peace?

Talk about how on 11 November people in the UK and elsewhere often wear poppies to remember those who have died during conflicts and wars. Do you know why poppies were chosen as a symbol?

I wonder… do you have a family story about what happened during a war?

5. Emoji biscuits

You will need: plain biscuits (sweet or savoury); assorted cut-up fruit and vegetables; pretzels, mini breadsticks, etc.

Remember to risk assess for allergies and intolerances.

Can you make a happy face on your biscuit? Can you make it sad? Can you make it angry? Can you make an emoji for someone who is feeling at peace?

Talk about how you feel today. Why do our emotions change? What emotions might someone experiencing conflict feel? Tell me about your peace emoji – what did you do? What emotions did Jesus experience? (Remember, Jesus wept when his friend Lazarus died and he got angry in the temple.) How can Jesus help us?

I wonder… is it possible to be happy all the time?

6. Peace dove with happy faces

You will need: magazines; a large piece of paper; pens; glue; scissors

First, draw a large dove outline on the piece of paper (you can copy one from online to make this easier). Then, from the magazines find pictures of people smiling and stick them on to the large dove.

Talk about what would make the world a better place. How can you make your part of the world (your home, your classroom, your office or place of work) a more peaceful and happier place?

I wonder… what difference could a smile make to someone you meet? Do you think God smiles at you?

7. Shaving foam marbling

You will need: shallow trays; cans of shaving foam; food colouring (that can be dripped one drop at a time); cocktail sticks; paper (or card); a shower scraper; access to a sink for washing hands

Soap cleans things – dishes, clothes, our hands and more. Shake the can of shaving foam and spray carefully in a thin layer on to the tray. Add drops of different food colourings on to it. Swirl with a cocktail stick. Place a sheet of paper on top and press down gently. Lift off and scrape away the foam. You should have a lovely, marbled piece of paper. When it's dry, try making it into a card or use as wrapping paper.

Talk about whether there is a person that you need to make peace with. Perhaps you could make them a card out of the marbled paper. Is there a small gift or 'peace offering' you could give with it, using the marbled paper as gift wrap?

I wonder… did you know that something beautiful could come from a mess? How can God make our messes into something beautiful?

8. Peace flags 

> **You will need: white fabric pieces (approximately 16 x 25 cm); smooth stones (or hammers if you prefer); green juicy leaves; sticks or straws**

Fold the fabric in half. Place a leaf or two in between. Bang with a stone or hammer until you can see the green colour come through the fabric. Unfold. Attach a straw or stick to the short end. Decorate with felt tips if you wish. Plant in your garden – and wave carefully!

Talk about how the white flag is an internationally recognised protective sign of truce or ceasefire, for negotiation and for surrender. Abigail didn't use a white flag – she took food and supplies to the enemy. She negotiated with David by talking with him. Is there someone you need to talk with and listen to? God always listens to us, but sometimes we have to surrender/give up what we want to what he knows is best for us.

I wonder… what are we prepared to surrender or give up? Jesus surrendered to death on the cross so that we might have eternal life with him.

9. Peace prayer dove

> **You will need: a straw; a paper dove shape (you can easily find templates online); a small paper rectangle; tape; pencils/pens**

Wrap the paper rectangle around the straw (not too tight) and then fold the top of the paper over to make a 'pocket' for the end of the straw. Make sure that there is a little gap between the fold of the pocket and the end of the straw, or your paper will stick to the straw and will not fly when the time comes!

Write or draw prayers for people or places who need God's peace on the front of the dove shape. Turn the dove over and tape the paper pocket to it. Turn the dove the right way round, aim it and then blow through the straw. Watch your peace dove fly as a symbol of giving the prayers to God!

Talk about why a dove is used as a symbol of peace. Jesus said to his disciples just before he was to be taken away to be tried and crucified: 'Peace I leave with you; my peace I give you' (John 14:27). Does this help you to be a peacemaker?

I wonder… is there a right or wrong way to pray? Do you find 'action' prayers easier?

10. Where in the world?

> **You will need: a large map; Lego or Playmobil people; lists about persecuted Christians in different countries across the world and their stories (Open Doors is one charity that has lots of resources, just look at their website)**

Abigail's husband was at war. The Bible describes him as a wicked man, who did not care for others, unlike his wife Abigail, the peacemaker. Read some of the stories of persecuted Christians facing difficult situations. Identify countries and, as you place a person on the map, thank God for the countries and Christians there.

Talk about what war means. What does persecution mean? Why was Abigail able to stand up for what was right?

I wonder… would you be like Abigail and stand up for what is right? I wonder how you would cope if you were being persecuted for being a follower of Jesus?

Celebration

Gather everyone for the celebration. Start by finding out what people have discovered through the activities.

We're going to start off by watching this video all about the story of Abigail (**youtu.be/K0Z0wt4Geb8**).

If you don't have access to the internet then you could re-enact the story:

There was a very rich man named Nabal living in the desert. He had 1,000 goats and 3,000 sheep. David and the men in his army were hungry from running from King Saul, so David sent a messenger to ask Nabal to give David and his army some food. But Nabal refused to give any food!

The messengers came back to David and told him that Nabal wouldn't give them any food. David was angry that Nabal wouldn't give him any food. He was so angry, he said, 'I'm going to go kill Nabal!' David was doing the wrong thing. In his anger, he was going to kill Nabal.

But then, Nabal's wife came to see David. Her name was Abigail. Abigail said, 'David, please forgive Nabal. He was mean not to give you some food. Look, I brought some food for you and your army. Please don't kill Nabal.' She gave the food as a peace offering. Then, David felt peace in his heart, and he said, 'Abigail, thank you. I didn't want to kill Nabal. I just lost my temper. Now that you were thoughtful and brought us some food, that makes me feel better. I won't hurt Nabal. You have stopped me from killing someone and taking revenge today.'

When Abigail went home, Nabal was drunk from alcohol, and she didn't tell him that she had taken food to David and his army. The next morning, though, she did tell Nabal. Nabal was angry with Abigail for taking David some food. He was still a mean man. But then Nabal had a heart attack, and he died. After Nabal died, Abigail married David.

After you've finished the video or done the reenactment say:

The thing that made all the difference in the end was that Abigail reminded David of who he was in the eyes of God and who he would become one day: 'You fight the Lord's battles… the Lord… has appointed him ruler over Israel, my lord will not have on his conscience the staggering burden of needless bloodshed or of having avenged himself' (1 Samuel 25:27–31, NIV)

As a result, David changes his mind and puts down his weapons. He said, 'Blessed be the Lord… who sent you to meet me today! Blessed be your good sense' (1 Samuel 25:32–33, NRSV).

A thousand years later, Jesus encouraged people to be peacemakers, when he spoke to thousands of people on a hillside. He said: 'Blessed are the peacemakers, for they will be called children of God' (Matthew 5:9, NIV).

I wonder…

- How do we make a difference in our lives and in those of others?
- How can I make and keep peace?
- What am I prepared to give up for Jesus?

Prayer

Using the flying peace prayer doves, pray for: the world, especially war-torn countries; your own country and people who govern us; your local area; your family; your Messy Church.

Song suggestions

- 'Let there be peace on earth' – Jill Jackson-Miller and Sy Miller
- 'I've got peace like a river' – Cedarmont Kids
- 'Everlasting peace' – iSingPOP
- 'As one' – Mark and Helen Johnson (Out of the Ark Music)
- 'Remembrance song' – Songs for Schools
- 'This is the day' – iSingPOP

Meal suggestions

Make a feast like Abigail took to David. Abigail's feast included 200 loaves of bread, wine, meat, roasted grain, raisin and fig cakes (1 Samuel 25:18). You might like to choose something more appropriate for your local Messy Church! For example, if you're serving breakfast, this could include: watermelon, yogurts, chocolate brioche rolls, chocolate-filled croissants, anything on the firepit, bacon sandwiches, assorted cereals.

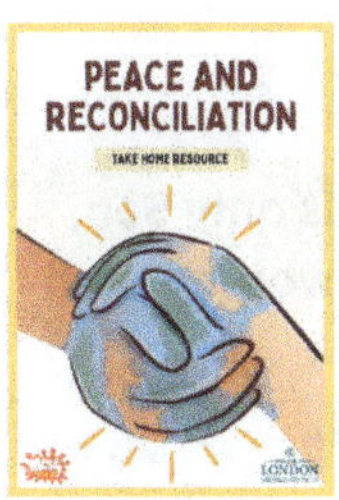

Have you seen our resource on peace and reconciliation? It's designed to support thoughtful conversations on this topic in ways accessible to all ages: **messychurch.brf.org.uk/resources/ peace-and-reconciliation.**

Session material: December
Joy to the WHOLE world!
by Johannah Myers and Jillian Mayer

Bible story for prep

Luke 1:26–38 (CEB)

When Elizabeth was six months pregnant, God sent the angel Gabriel to Nazareth, a city in Galilee, to a virgin who was engaged to a man named Joseph, a descendant of David's house. The virgin's name was Mary. When the angel came to her, he said, 'Rejoice, favoured one! The Lord is with you!' She was confused by these words and wondered what kind of greeting this might be. The angel said, 'Don't be afraid, Mary. God is honouring you. Look! You will conceive and give birth to a son, and you will name him Jesus. He will be great and he will be called the Son of the Most High. The Lord God will give him the throne of David his father. He will rule over Jacob's house forever, and there will be no end to his kingdom.'

Then Mary said to the angel, 'How will this happen since I haven't had sexual relations with a man?'

The angel replied, 'The Holy Spirit will come over you and the power of the Most High will overshadow you. Therefore, the one who is to be born will be holy. He will be called God's Son. Look, even in her old age, your relative Elizabeth has conceived a son. This woman who was labelled "unable to conceive" is now six months pregnant. Nothing is impossible for God.'

Then Mary said, 'I am the Lord's servant. Let it be with me just as you have said.' Then the angel left her.

John 3:16 (CEB)

God so loved the world that he gave his only Son, so that everyone who believes in him won't perish but will have eternal life.

Pointers

- What does the angel Gabriel tell Mary about who Jesus will be? Imagine being in Mary's shoes. How might you have reacted? How does Gabriel reassure Mary?
- God gave the whole world a gift when God gave Jesus to us. If you could give the whole world a gift, what would you give?

How does this session help people grow in Christ?

The nativity story is a powerful reminder of God's love and the joy that Christ's birth brings to the world. By reflecting on how the arrival of Jesus brought hope to **all** people, this session deepens our understanding of God's faithfulness. As we grasp the magnitude of this moment – God coming to earth as a child to save humanity – it can strengthen our trust in God's plan for our lives. The joy of the nativity story fills us with renewed faith, knowing that God's love is for **everyone**, offering peace and salvation to the entire world, not just the people that we know.

Add value

Mealtime card

- What brings you the most joy during the Advent/Christmas season?
- It's easy to think about what we want for Christmas or what our plans are to celebrate. How can we remember that Christmas is good news for the WHOLE world?
- What's one Christmas tradition from another country or culture that you admire?

Question to start and end the session

So… how can we share the joy of Jesus with others during the Advent and Christmas season – and throughout the year?

Social action idea

One activity calls for decorating gift bags that folks can take home and fill with food for local food banks. Encourage folks to fill their bags and return them at a designated time/place so that your Messy Church can help your local community.

Activities

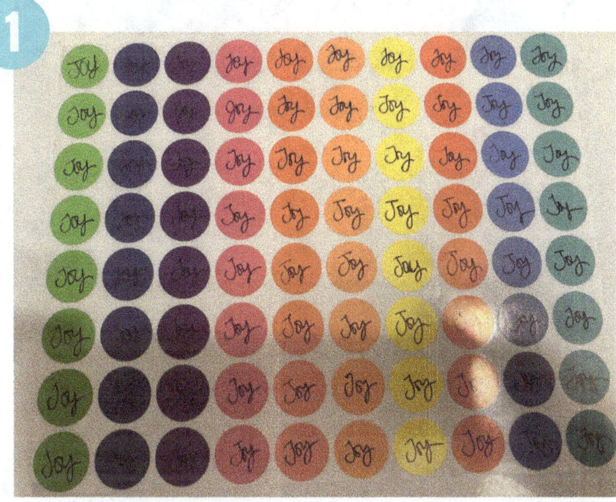

1. Contagious joy

You will need: several sheets of different coloured dot stickers with the word 'joy' written on each dot; scissors

Cut each sheet of stickers so that each participant has a line of joy stickers of the same colour. Hand a set of coloured stickers to each participant. When everyone is ready to begin, have a leader start the game. The game is essentially one of tag with the goal of spreading as much joy as possible during a set time frame (a few minutes, but depending on the space available it could be longer or shorter). So, once the leader starts the game, participants run around trying to stick a joy sticker on the other players. Once the leader calls time, everyone looks to see who has spread the most joy by counting the coloured dot stickers (if one player successfully sticks four yellow stickers on the other players while the players with blue and green stickers only stick three, the player with the yellow stickers would be the winner.)

Talk about how, like many things (flu viruses, yawns and smiles), joy can be quite contagious. Share what brings you joy.

I wonder... how can you be generous and spread joy throughout your world?

2. Gingerbread playdough 

You will need: ingredients for gingerbread playdough (see below); cookie/biscuit cutters in Christmas shapes; small rolling pins or other playdough toys

Ingredients:

- 120 g plain flour
- 150 g salt
- 150 ml water
- 1 tsp ground ginger
- 1 tsp ground cinnamon
- 1 tsp ground nutmeg
- 1 tsp ground cloves
- 2 tbsp cream of tartar
- 2 tbsp vegetable oil
- 1 tbsp cornflour

Make the playdough ahead of time by combining all the ingredients for the playdough into a microwave-safe bowl, stirring until combined. While microwave times may vary, the recipe suggests starting with one minute at regular power then stirring. Microwave for an additional 30 seconds and then stir. Finish the dough by kneading by hand (after it cools sufficiently).

When it's made, use the various cutters and shapes to make different figures and designs, etc. Be as creative as you like!

Talk about how this playdough smells Christmasy. What other smells remind you of Christmas? Why does Christmas make us feel happy or joyful? The smell of gingerbread or other Christmas scents fill up the whole house or room. How can we fill our community with the joy of Christmas?

I wonder... how can we remember the joy of God's gift of Jesus at Christmas all year long?

3. Angel ornament

You will need: white paper (A4); scissors; string; wooden beads; a glue stick or double-sided tape; pens/pencils (optional)

With the paper landscape, fold into an accordion fan (use a video online if you need help), then cut it in half. Fold each half a third of the way down to make arms/wings. Attach a wooden bead to a piece of string to make the angel's head, creating a loop at the top of the bead to use to hang the angel ornament. Glue the string between the two sides of the angel. If you'd like, decorate the angel too.

Talk about how the angel brought Mary good news for the whole world, the news of Jesus' coming. But that news was shocking and even a little scary. How can good news also be a little scary? How can you be a messenger of good news like the angel Gabriel and share the good news of Jesus in your community?

I wonder… what do you think the angel looked like? How did Mary feel when she saw the angel?

4. Repeat the sounding joy cards

You will need: blank cards and envelopes; pens/coloured pencils/markers; a thesaurus/dictionary/translation tool or access to these online

Create a Christmas card to send to someone this Christmas season by creating a joy word cloud. Write the word joy in big letters on the front of the card and then add words surrounding it that have a similar meaning (e.g. jubilation, glee) or are a translation of it – e.g. alegría (Spanish), freude (German). Get creative with the colours and fonts you use in writing the words. Once the word cloud is completed, write a note inside to bring someone joy during this holiday season.

Talk about how Jesus brought joy to the whole world when he was born! While you might not be able to bring joy to everyone on this planet, you can definitely bring joy to at least one person. What are some ways in addition to sending cards that you can bring joy to others?

I wonder… how can you bring joy to others the way that Jesus brought joy to the world when he was born?

5. Edible manger scene

You will need: thin pretzel sticks; animal-shaped crackers/biscuits; a biscuit that can be used to represent baby Jesus

Remember to risk assess for allergies and intolerances.

Use the pretzel sticks to 'build' a manger scene, adding animal crackers to help fill in your scene.

Talk about how Mary and Joseph were simple, ordinary people. When Jesus was born, he was placed in a manger, where animals might have eaten their food. Gabriel told Mary that Jesus would be king of a kingdom that would never end. Is it surprising that this baby who would be king was born in a stable to ordinary people? Can you think of a really great gift you've received that was simple or ordinary?

I wonder… what does Jesus' humble birth tell us about who God is and what God values?

6. Building Bethlehem

You will need: Lego or other building blocks

Build the Christmas story. Where are Mary and Joseph? Where is Mary's house? Where are you in the story?

Talk about how the angel made it clear to Mary that the good news of Jesus was good news for all the world. We are all a part of the joyous news of God sending his Son to live with us!

I wonder… if you were in this nativity story, which character would you be and why?

7. Follow the angel scavenger hunt

You will need: printed copies of the angel shaped cut-outs with scripture and discussion questions on them; a small prize for those who find all the clues which can serve to remind them of the nativity story, such as a small angel ornament

Set up a treasure hunt where participants follow angel-shaped clues to find parts of a nativity scene or symbols of the nativity story. Each clue includes a verse or question about a piece of the story. The last angel should be placed above a representation of baby Jesus, either life-size or from a playset.

Talk about how the journey you took to find all the angels mirrors that of Mary, who followed God's instructions and plan. Mary found joy and fulfilment when she gave birth to Jesus. Similarly, we find that seeking Jesus brings joy and fulfilment into our own lives.

I wonder… how did Mary feel when she first knew she was carrying Jesus in her womb?

8. Nature nativity scene

You will need: various leaves, sticks, rocks and other materials from outside (or have Messy participants do this themselves); optional supplies could be paper and glue/tape if people are making individual nativity scenes to take home

Using the materials gifted to us by God's creation all around, create a manger scene. This could be something created by the whole group or individually.

Talk about how God's gifts for us are all around. We see God's love through us in the beauty of nature. God loves every part of the world God created, not just humans! So Jesus' birth was good news for the WHOLE world.

I wonder… how did the whole of creation celebrate Jesus' birth?

9. Joy in the stars above community prayer art

You will need: a bulletin board, canvas or large sheet of paper with the nativity scene depicted in the bottom section (this could be a basic drawing, a glued-on image from the internet, or even the front of a recycled Christmas card); paint pens (yellow, white, gold, or silver)

Think of people, places and other things that bring you joy. For each thing, draw a star in the night sky and say a prayer of thanks to God for the gift of that person/place/thing.

Talk about how people all over the world, despite living miles apart, look at the same sky each night. The sky over Bethlehem when Jesus was born so many years ago is the same sky over Bethlehem today. Like our shared sky, the joy that Jesus brings is for everyone all over the world!

I wonder… what brings people joy in other places around the world? Are they the same things that bring us joy?

10. Greatest gift bag

You will need: blank paper gift bags or recycled cardboard boxes (one for every family unit); pens; stickers; other items to decorate the bags or boxes

Decorate the bag or box. Take it home with you and collect food for your local food bank. At the end of December, deliver your food so that it can help others in your community.

Talk about how God is always so generous with us – God is generous with love, with grace, with mercy. Christmas reminds us of how much God loves us – and the whole world. How can we practise God's generosity in our community?

I wonder… what one thing can you do to be more generous this Christmas?

Celebration

Today, we're celebrating the most incredible gift ever given: Jesus Christ. His birth is not just a story; it is the fulfilment of God's promise of love, a gift that brings joy to the entire world. Let's explore what this means!

What is the first thing that comes to mind when you think about Christmas? *Allow for responses – perhaps they mention family, gifts, traditions or joy.*

Let's take a moment to consider how the joyous Christmas story began for Mary, Jesus' mother. In Luke 1, we meet her when she is visited by the angel Gabriel. *Read Luke 1:26–38 aloud.*

When the angel appeared to Mary, what were the first words spoken? 'Rejoice, favoured one! The Lord is with you!' This is a message of joy. Even though Mary was troubled and unsure, God's message was clear: God's plan was one of hope and joy, for her and for the whole world. Mary was chosen to carry Jesus, and her 'yes' brought the beginning of joy to the world.

What do you think Mary felt when the angel told her this news? What would you have felt?

Encourage participants to discuss their answers in small groups. If time permits, allow for groups to share their responses.

The joy of Jesus' birth isn't just for Mary or even just for the people of Israel. It's for the whole world! In John 3:16, we hear how big God's love is. Let's read this verse together. I'll start, and you can join in. *Read John 3:16 together. If possible, have the verse visible on a poster/display at the front of the room.*

This very important piece of scripture tells us the 'why' of Christmas. Jesus is God's ultimate gift of love. He was sent to bring joy, not just to a few, but to everyone, everywhere. Jesus' birth is the beginning of that joy – because it brings salvation, hope and love to the world.

This joy that we've been talking about isn't meant to stay with us; it's meant to be shared. Just like Mary shared the joy of Jesus with the world, we are called to share that joy too. Christmas reminds us that God's love is for everyone, and our response should be to reflect that love and joy in our lives.

How can we bring the joy of Jesus to others, especially during the Christmas season?

Invite people to share their ideas. Suggestions might include acts of kindness, service or sharing their faith with others.

Jesus' birth is more than just a holiday event; it's the fulfilment of God's promise of love. This is why we celebrate Christmas with joy. As we sing, share and give during this season, let's remember the joy that came into the world through Jesus – joy that brings hope, love and salvation to all who believe.

Let's take a moment to think of someone in your life who needs the joy of Jesus. Think of ways that you can share God's love with them this week. Let's pray and ask God to help us spread the joy of Christ this Christmas season.

I wonder...

- How the world would be impacted if all people challenged themselves to spread joy this Christmas season?
- Who most needs to hear a message of joy this Christmas season?
- What can you do to spread joy in your own part of the world?

Prayer

God of joy, thank you for the gift of your Son, Jesus. As we celebrate his birth, help us to carry this joy into the world, sharing your love with everyone we meet. Amen.

Song suggestions

- 'Joy to the world'
- 'Angels we have heard on high'
- 'Hark! The herald angels sing'
- 'A child in a manger born' – Mark and Helen Johnson (Out of the Ark Music)
- 'Hear the bells' – Nick and Becky Drake (Worship for Everyone)
- 'The gift' – iSingPOP

Meal suggestions

Create a menu that includes different foods from around the world or that features foods enjoyed by Christians around the world at Christmas, such as: barbecue (Australia and South Africa), roast turkey (United States), roast goose (Great Britain and Germany), a julbord, which includes cold cuts, fish, sausage and cheese (Sweden), tamales (Mexico) and yule log cake (France).

Session material: January
Perseverance: following Jesus takes practice
by Greg Ross with illustrations by Andrew McDonough

Bible story for prep

Luke 15:1–7 (MSG)

By this time a lot of men and women of questionable reputation were hanging around Jesus, listening intently. The Pharisees and religion scholars were not pleased, not at all pleased. They growled, 'He takes in sinners and eats meals with them, treating them like old friends.' Their grumbling triggered this story.

'Suppose one of you had a hundred sheep and lost one. Wouldn't you leave the ninety-nine in the wilderness and go after the lost one until you found it? When found, you can be sure you would put it across your shoulders, rejoicing, and when you got home call in your friends and neighbours, saying, "Celebrate with me! I've found my lost sheep!" Count on it – there's more joy in heaven over one sinner's rescued life than over ninety-nine good people in no need of rescue.'

Pointers

Some people think that if they choose to follow the way of Jesus, their life will be simple and easy. The stories of the first followers of Jesus in our Bibles teach us that those first women and men heard a lesson and then had a chance to put the lesson into practice. Many times they failed or made mistakes or doubted and questioned Jesus' teaching. Then they had to go back and keep practising again and again. All through history the people of God have shared this reality in stories, song, prayers and artwork as ways to keep encouraging new followers to keep on going and not to give up when it gets hard or they make mistakes, to persevere.

How does this session help people grow in Christ?

This session is designed to help people of all ages learn that following the way of Jesus requires lots of practice. This means having a go, failing sometimes, having another go and learning better ways, and keeping on. In other words, living the way of Jesus requires perseverance, and it's better shared in a group or community.

Add value

Mealtime card

- Share one thing that you have had to do lots of practice to be good at. It might be tying your shoe laces or a craft or sport or learning an instrument or something else.

- Share a story about your favourite party that you have been to. What made it feel so special that you remember it?

- What do you know about sheep, shepherds and sheep dogs in your country?

Question to start and end the session

So… who has showed you how to follow the way of Jesus? How can you help others to practise following Jesus and encourage them to persevere as followers of Jesus?

Social action idea

Taking care of the environment takes lots of perseverance. We have a Clean Up Australia Day on the first Sunday in March each year. Find out when your national/regional clean up event is and plan to take part. Make sure you do a risk assessment and have the necessary safety gear, i.e. gloves, hats, bags, and have a social time afterwards. Start with a prayer as a commitment to being part of Jesus' prayer that 'the kingdom of heaven may come on earth'.

Activities

1. Fitness challenge

You will need: a five station fitness challenge set up with options for people of different ages and abilities

Depending on the weather in your part of the world, you could choose to have an outdoor or indoor five station fitness challenge. These could be team or individual challenges. Keep a record of who wins at each station, or you could give out points for coming first, second, third and so on. Possible stations could be:

- Weight lifting. Using sets of 1–5 kg weights or bags containing tinned foods, see who can lift the weights the most times within 30 seconds.

- Set up a sheet of blank paper on a wall and give each participant a piece of colour chalk and get them to have up to three goes at jumping their highest and making a mark on the wall.

- Get each person to make a paper plane and see who can get their plane to fly the farthest. Three trial flights each and keep a record.

- Sit/stand ups. See who can do the most sit ups in 30 seconds. For people with different abilities this may need to be standing up from a seated position or another appropriate challenge.

- Skipping challenge. Have a number of different length skipping ropes for different ages and heights. See how many 'skips of the rope' each person can do without stopping in 30 seconds.

Talk about how fitness for all sport requires lots of training sessions, sometimes individually and sometimes as a team, depending on the sport. We will have good training sessions and bad training sessions. Sometimes we might not feel like going to training, but we know that if we don't then we won't improve or we will let the coach/team down. Following Jesus is very similar. It is much easier to follow Jesus when we do that with someone else, which

is why churches and Messy Church happens. People get together to learn and practise following Jesus based on the five core values of Messy Church (Christ-centred, for all ages, creativity, hospitality and celebration).

I wonder… what have you learned about following Jesus at Messy Church? Could you teach that to someone else older or younger than you?

2. Perseverance in nature

You will need: pictures of animals, birds and insects that keep going when we think it may be too much (e.g. birds that migrate, dogs/cats walking home after getting lost, ants that build huge mounds); craft materials to make simple dogs/cats/insects/birds (e.g. cardboard tubes, pipe cleaner stick, tissue paper, tape, etc.); list of names that mean strong, brave, wise, fearless

Create an animal or insect that reflects the quality 'perseverance' using the craft materials available. Get them to choose a name for their creation.

Talk about how God is the source of all life and every life teaches us about perseverance. Tell one or two stories about animals that persevere in the face of challenges, e.g. flocks of birds flying through storms over oceans with no places to rest or eat or drink on their way to their destination or dolphins who work together to catch fish for their family which they could not do if they only fished on their own. You will find plenty of examples on the internet.

There were many times when Jesus could have given up on his earthly mission. However, he kept going because he loved his friends, and they learned how to persevere when they faced lots of problems and challenges. In today's Bible story, Jesus tells a story about a shepherd who perseveres in looking for a lost sheep. What does this tell us about the nature of God?

I wonder… what animals do you know about that inspire you to keep going when you want to give up?

3. Macramé keyring 

You will need: 5 mm think single strand cotton macramé chord in different colours (each key ring will need two 33" pieces and one 15" piece); a keychain ring with lobster craft; scissors; a comb; instructions for making a macrame keyring (following a video on YouTube might be easiest – youtu.be/ gD0B47-tKjc)

Have the video available and let people have a go making keychains. You could also demonstrate the knots and steps and then encourage people to try, and perhaps even having to undo knots and then start again. The big thing with macramé is starting and finishing well, so that the finished product lasts and does not come undone.

Talk about how we learn about following Jesus from all the wonderful people who have their stories written down in our Bibles and from all the stories that have been collected in the 2,000 years since Jesus was on earth. Like making macramé, to follow Jesus we need to have someone show us or tell us how to start, and then we need instructions to get on and be a follower of Jesus. Sometimes we make mistakes and have to go back and learn things again, and that is okay. Sometimes it can seem like we will never get the thing we are trying to do right, and we might want to give up or walk away from that activity or challenge.

God never holds our mistakes against us if we are honest about them, say sorry and work to improve and do better from that point on. Jesus describes God to be like a shepherd who perseveres in looking for a sheep that's wandered off. When the sheep is found, the shepherd carries it home and celebrates that the lost sheep is found. What does this tell us about God?

I wonder… how do you feel about reading and/or following steps or instructions? Do you like to follow steps, or do you prefer to work it out on your own by having a go, working out what went wrong and having another go? Making macramé might seem old fashioned and so can following Jesus. Who could encourage you to keep going with your faith?

4. Perseverance acrostic poem

You will need: A4 sheets of paper printed with the word PERSEVERANCE down the left-hand side; pens

Invite people to create an acrostic poem about Messy Church or following Jesus using the first letters for each line from the letters printed down the left-hand side of the paper. The lines can be just one word or a whole sentence. The poems can be funny or serious or a mix of both. When they are finished, with permission, take a copy of them and share them later or have them printed and given to people at the next Messy Church.

Talk about how lots of people love words, while others find writing and reading really hard. It's similar for people when they think about following Jesus. If you love words then this activity is for you. It's also an activity that can be shared by all ages. Some people may be good with words or rhyming and need someone to be the person who writes it down for them. Some people can do this quickly; other people need quite a bit of time. It's the same with learning to follow Jesus: some people seem to pick it up quickly and others really struggle. That is where learning to follow Jesus with other people is so important. They can help us persevere.

I wonder… what do you like to read? What's your favourite Bible story or prayer? Make a list to share on your Messy Church social media or newsletter. This is a good opportunity to find out if people have their own Bible and would like one as a gift.

5. Ice cream in a bag 

You will need: ½ cup heavy whipping cream; 1 tbsp caster or icing sugar; ¼ tsp vanilla essence; 3 cups crushed ice; 1/3 cup rock salt; 2–3 litre ziplock bag; sandwich ziplock bag

Remember to risk assess for allergies and intolerances.

Make your ice cream:

- Add heavy whipping cream, caster sugar or icing sugar and vanilla in the sandwich bag. Seal the bag completely.

- Add crushed ice and rock salt to the 3-litre bag.

- Put the smaller bag inside the larger bag. Seal the bag completely.

- Shake until ice cream is formed – 5–10 minutes.

- Enjoy your ice cream

Talk about what it means to persevere. Generally, it means to keep working at something even when it may not look like it is working or you are doing this by yourself. Making ice cream in a bag takes a lot of perseverance to keep mixing and shaking and mixing and shaking until the mixture changes from cream and sugar and vanilla into proper yummy ice cream.

I wonder… how long do you think it will take to make the mixture become ice cream? I wonder how you have shown perseverance or sticking to something that may have been difficult this week?

6. Holding prayer cross

You will need: pre-cut wooden crosses; sand paper of various grades; wood wax or oil; rags

With your store of precut crosses from different timbers, invite people to choose one that they like. You may have some pre-waxed or oiled so they know what they will look like finished. Provide two or three grades of sand paper and invite people to start and sand off the rough parts until the cross is lovely and smooth to touch. Wipe down with a dust or tac cloth and then provide them with wax or oil to seal the grain.

Talk about how long it would have taken your wood worker to cut out all the rough crosses and how much longer it might take to sand and smooth and oil or wax. Ask them how long it takes people to learn things. Some scientists say it takes 10,000 hours of practice to become good at something. Talk about how Jesus had just three years with his friends to teach them how to live God's way, and then they had to keep on practising for the rest of their lives. Sometimes following Jesus can feel like having the rough parts of our personality sanded back and smoothed off until what we do and say are more like Jesus. The work of the Holy Spirit can be like the wax or oil that keeps us the way Jesus wants us to be.

I wonder… how long does it take for people to become really good at following the way of Jesus?

7. Pancake tossing 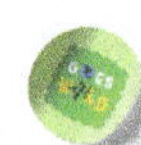

You will need: a selection of similar-sized pancake pans; a good stock of pancakes made a day or two before; score sheet for judge/s to assess the height pancake is tossed, whether it is caught cleanly in the pan and how much style or dancing is shown by the participant

Cooking is a skill that takes lots and lots of practice. So is the art of cooking a pancake, tossing it in the air and catching it again without making a mess. We are not going to toss raw or half-cooked pancakes. We are going to toss cooked pancakes and see how much practice we might need to put in before Pancake or Shrove Tuesday. Mark out an area that up to five people can compete in safely. Appoint two judges or adjudicators, give them the score-sheet and get them to keep score. Give each participant a couple of practice turns and then take their best of three scores. You may want to run it in age ranges, depending on your Messy Church. Get people to cheer each other on and encourage each other.

Talk about how some people think that following Jesus is all boring and following rules, but following Jesus can also be lots of fun. Learning to laugh at ourselves when we make mistakes is important. Encouraging others when they mess up or have a down day or can't get it together is also really important. Spending time together working but also playing is also a really special part of belonging to Jesus' family, especially at Messy Church. Jesus told lots and lots of wonderful stories or parables that are full of humour and jokes that we often miss – like imagining a camel trying to get through the eye of a needle. Just like pancake tossing, following Jesus requires a lot of practice and it also needs our church family to cheer us on and teach us better ways to toss our pancakes or follow Jesus.

I wonder… who has shown you that following Jesus can be lots of fun? What can you do to show others that following Jesus can be fun?

8. The colours of creation 

You will need: a sheet of paper and a clipboard for each person; selection of water colour pencils; water; paint brushes; a place to hang the pictures as they dry

If you can take your group outside, invite them to sit somewhere and with the water colour pencils draw something from nature that demonstrates perseverance or commitment. This could be a plant growing in a crack, ants running to their nest, baby birds being taught how to fly or insects gathering honey. Then with a small amount of water use the paint brush to go over the drawing and you will create a water colour effect painting.

If you cannot go outside, provide a selection of 10–20 images of creatures from around your region that show tenacity. In Western Australia we have the tiniest orchids that grow in the wild. They are so small that when walking in the bush you can easily stand on them. But when you stop and look, the beauty and structure are jaw dropping. Their tenacity and perseverance in growing is astounding. There are other plants in Australia whose seeds only germinate when two essential ingredients from smoke land on them. Find some pictures of wild things from your part of creation and encourage people to draw and then paint those or to draw something from memory they have seen.

Talk about how every part of creation is different and unique because each has developed to suit its natural surroundings and climate. It is the same way with Messy Church around the world. Every Messy Church is unique. Some countries have their own names that better reflect the five core values of Messy Church for their culture and language. It is also the same for people who follow Jesus around the world. The church around the world sings, prays and reads the Bible in thousands of different languages. People also follow Jesus in different ways. Some go to church on Saturday, others on Fridays or Sundays. Some don't eat meat, others don't have music in their churches, others wear special clothes to go to church and others go just as they are. The important thing is that someone in their community is helping them to follow Jesus where they are.

I wonder… what can our Messy Church do to persevere and keep on sharing the story of Jesus?

9. Prayer beads

You will need: some larger beads of different colours or shapes and sizes; some fishing line, dental floss or bead string; clasps if desired; multiple copies of well-known prayers or Bible verses (e.g. the Lord's Prayer, the Messy Blessing, the beatitudes, well-known Bible verses, etc.); a hole punch/stapler

Make sure you have multiple copies of different prayers/ verses. Invite people to choose 5–10 of the prayers or verses. Punch or staple them together into a little booklet and then choose a different kind of bead for each prayer that will remind them of that prayer. Turn the beads into a bracelet/chain using the strong and clasp. People can use the booklet for as long as they like until they learn the prayers or verses from memory, and they become part of their daily routine, e.g. saying them when getting up or going to bed. People might also like to use beads with a letter on them to help them remember the first words of the prayer or the first letter of the name of someone they want to pray for every day.

Talk about how you learned to pray or how you learned to remember the words of the Lord's Prayer or the Messy Blessing or other well-loved prayers or Bible verses. Share

how you take time to pray. Sometimes praying can be hard and we might not be so good with words. That is when it is really helpful to have prayers that people who are great with words have written. In time we will get better at praying and feel more comfortable creating and praying our own prayers alongside those that others have written.

I wonder… when do you pray the most? What kind of prayers do you like or find helpful? What stops you from praying?

10. Songs from around the world

You will need: one or two songs about following Jesus that are sung in churches around the world

Get one of the people in your area to write out the words for the song 'Jesus loves me' or another popular hymn in another language that may be used in your area. For example, in south-west Western Australia we would be learning this in Nyoongar Wardandi language. In other parts of the world there will similarly be first people's languages that until recently were silenced; many first peoples would have been beaten or jailed if they were heard speaking their own language. Learn the chorus of 'Jesus loves me' in these words, and share it in the celebration.

As the good news about Jesus has spread all around the world, the Bible has been translated into the languages of almost every nation. Many songs and hymns have been the way that people who did not know reading or writing in their language learned long parts of the Bible and the stories about Jesus.

Talk about how, in Australia, German missionaries came to central Australia in the early days of white settlement and lived among the first peoples there. The country was so different from their home country and the culture was completely foreign. They practised and practised learning the local people's languages, carefully writing them down sound by sound and word by word so that they could share the good news of Jesus in the local people's language. They also worked hard and translated many of their Lutheran hymns into their languages. This was a commitment to truly serve the first people's communities. Then things changed, and many of the songs were thought lost. In the last decade the Central Australian Women's Choir has reformed. Through the careful work of these first German missionaries, many of these women have been able to learn their own ancient language and reconnect with the deep truths about Jesus. They have travelled back to Germany and around the world, singing the hymns in their own language and sharing the wonderful news about Jesus.

I wonder… how long would you be willing to learn and practise another language so that you could tell the good news of Jesus to people who may have never heard of him?

Celebration

Use Andrew McDonough's 'Cecil the Lost Sheep' story to retell the story Jesus told about a lost sheep in Luke 15:1–7. The shepherd shows so much perseverance by firstly following Cecil and then bringing him home again. Download the PowerPoint from the log on details provided in this resource, and show the images on a big screen as the story is told. Work with someone to help you learn the story from memory and tell it with as much enthusiasm and different voices as you can, as this makes such a difference! Alternatively you could get one or two people to 'play' the characters in the story or invite everyone in the celebration to do the actions of Cecil and the Shepherd with you.

I wonder…

- What do you like best about this story?
- What questions do you have about this story?
- What helps you to keep going in your faith?

Prayer

Use one or more of the perseverance acrostic poems that have been created as the basis for a time of prayer.

Song suggestions

- 'I have decided to follow Jesus' – Simon Kara Marak
- 'What a friend we have in Jesus'

- 'I see God in you' – Heather Price
- 'Sunshine on a rainy day' – iSingPOP
- 'Change and grow' – Mark and Helen Johnson (Out of the Ark Music)
- 'Resilience in me' – Songs for Schools
- 'Messy Church Song' by Greg Ross, to the tune of 'The Wellerman' (a New Zealand folk song). Tune is in public domain.

Verse 1 If you want to know God and have some fun –
Meet friends, eat food, create 'til we're done
Messy Church is the place for you
You are weclome in this place

Chorus Welcome to Messy Church
Come in, have a drink and find your perch
Welcome to one and all
This is the Jesus way (huh)

Verse 2 If you're by yourself or feel alone
Come in and find yourself a home
All shapes and sizes, old and young
You are welcome in this place

Verse 3 Jesus is the guy to know
His love and wisdom are the go
We tell his stories, sing great songs
You are welcome in this place

Verse 4 Folks of all ages can be friends
and learn and play the Jesus way
We work together, change the world
God is working in our mess (huh)

Meal suggestions

Have a celebration feast using whatever foods your community has when it celebrates. For some communities it may be a barbecue or grill; for other communities it may be a roast dinner with all the trimmings; for others it may be a special treat to have pizza or fish and chips or other 'take away treat' meals. The idea is to remind people of the commitment of the shepherd to finding the sheep that was lost and then celebrating that with a feast for all their friends. Make sure people know ahead of time to invite their friends to this special feast. Alternatively, you could invite everyone to bring enough of their favourite celebration food for themselves and a little to share for a 'pot luck' meal.

Session material: February
Love: how does this grow?
By Helen Laird

 **SUPPORT MATERIAL**    **MESSY CHURCH AT HOME**    **MESSY CHURCH GOES WILD**

Bible story for prep

Luke 15:11–32 (ICB)

Then Jesus said, 'A man had two sons. The younger son said to his father, "Give me my share of the property." So the father divided the property between his two sons. Then the younger son gathered up all that was his and left. He travelled far away to another country. There he wasted his money in foolish living. He spent everything that he had. Soon after that, the land became very dry, and there was no rain. There was not enough food to eat anywhere in the country. The son was hungry and needed money. So he got a job with one of the citizens there. The man sent the son into the fields to feed pigs. The son was so hungry that he was willing to eat the food the pigs were eating. But no one gave him anything. The son realised that he had been very foolish. He thought, "All of my father's servants have plenty of food. But I am here, almost dying with hunger. I will leave and return to my father. I'll say to him: Father, I have sinned against God and against you. I am not good enough to be called your son. But let me be like one of your servants." So the son left and went to his father.

'While the son was still a long way off, his father saw him coming. He felt sorry for his son. So the father ran to him, and hugged and kissed him. The son said, "Father, I have sinned against God and against you. I am not good enough to be called your son." But the father said to his servants, "Hurry! Bring the best clothes and put them on him. Also, put a ring on his finger and sandals on his feet. And get our fat calf and kill it. Then we can have a feast and celebrate! My son was dead, but now he is alive again! He was lost, but now he is found!" So they began to celebrate.

'The older son was in the field. As he came closer to the house, he heard the sound of music and dancing. So he called to one of the servants and asked, "What does all this mean?" The servant said, "Your brother has come back. Your father killed the fat calf to eat because your brother came home safely!" The older son was angry and would not go in to the feast. So his father went out and begged him to come in. The son said to his father, "I have served you like a slave for many years! I have always obeyed your commands. But you never even killed a young goat for me to have a feast with my friends. But your other son has wasted all your money on prostitutes. Then he comes home, and you kill the fat calf for him!" The father said to him, "Son, you are always with me. All that I have is yours. We had to celebrate and be happy because your brother was dead, but now he is alive. He was lost, but now he is found."'

Pointers

Luke 15:11–32 is a parable allowing us to be curious about what Jesus wanted us to learn about God. This session has been written around discovering God's big love for us, which in turn allows our love to shine through.

How does this session help people grow in Christ?

This session will help us to understand how to show love in all situations, whether people are kind or not. In the parable, it was as if the son asking for his father's money was saying, 'I want you dead'; yet when the son comes home, the father greets him with love and forgiveness. What does this story tell us about the nature of God?

Add value

Mealtime card

- When do you find it hard to show love?
- How do you show love to others?
- Who shows love to you and how?

Question to start and end the session

So… where is love?

Social action idea

Give an item each week to your local food bank.

Activities

1. Welcome

You will need: a large sheet of paper (or roll of lining paper); glue; writing/drawing pens; items to stick on for decoration (tissue paper, stars, stickers, etc.)

Use the items provided to create a large, bright welcome banner.

Talk about how the loving Father was so pleased to see his son he ran to greet him and hugged him. This was despite the fact that previously the son couldn't wait to get his hands on his father's money, and then when he did, he spent it unwisely.

I wonder… who are you pleased to see the most? What's the best welcome you have been given or received?

2. Money goes fast

You will need: coins; paper; wax crayons; cards with monetary amounts which can be made up from the available coins (e.g. £1.72 can be made up from £1, 50p, 20p, 2p)

Use the resources to make rubbings of the different values of the coins. You could then cut them out. This activity could be extended into a game. On a table have cards, turned face down, with monetary amounts on them that will take 3–5 coins to make the total. The competitors turn over a card and then race each other (or against a timer) to rub the coins **clearly** to make that total.

Talk about how the son couldn't wait to get his hands on his father's money, and then when he did, he spent it unwisely.

I wonder… if you have ever made an unwise purchase? Or bought something that later you regretted?

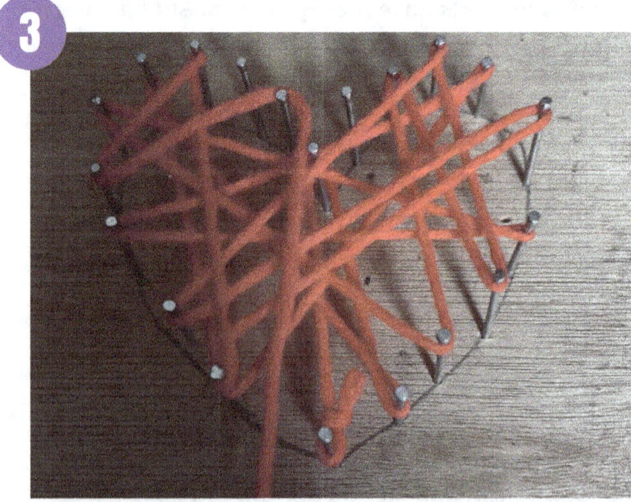

3. Loving through it

You will need: a piece of wood (c. 10 cm x 10 cm); nails; a hammer; long lengths of red or pink string/wool; a heart template; a pencil

Using the pencil draw around the heart template. Decide how many nails you want to use; ideally, you should use enough so that they are spaced 1.5–2 cm apart along the edge of the line you have drawn. Hammer in the nails where you have marked. Tie the end of the string to a nail and then either in order or randomly take the string across the heart shape and pass it around another nail. Keep moving the string around the heart shape until you are satisfied, then tie it off.

Talk about how God is an all-forgiving God. With God's help we can try to live the same way. When people hurt us (symbolised by the nails in the wood), we feel wounded, hurt and angry. God, like the father in this story, is ready to forgive us, and the more we learn to forgive, the easier it becomes. With the help of God's Spirit, we can learn to forgive like God does. Place this heart somewhere where you will see it to remind you to forgive just as God does.

I wonder… are there any situations where you need to forgive others? Or do you need to ask for forgiveness from someone else?

4. Breaking news 

> **You will need: pens; paper; copies of the Bible passage in two or three versions**

Read the Bible passage and then write a newspaper headline article or a social media post about the story, including all the drama and emotions.

Talk about how the news is often full of sad reports. Why is that? What would it feel like if a good news story, like a story of love and/or forgiveness, was always in the media?

I wonder… what good news story can you share?

5. Pig biscuits

> **You will need: plain biscuits; medium-sized marshmallows; pink wafer biscuits; chocolate drops or dried fruit; pink buttercream; a knife; named paper plates (or similar)**

Remember to risk assess for allergies and intolerances.

Use a knife to cover the biscuit with buttercream, add the marshmallow as the nose and small triangles of pink wafer biscuits as the ears, and then use chocolate drops or dried fruit for the eyes. You could add two small spots of buttercream on the marshmallow for the nostrils on your pig's nose.

Talk about how the son in our story today made a big mistake, ending up in the worst job possible for a Jew – feeding pigs! However, that did not stop his dad from loving him. You will eat this pig biscuit and then it will be gone, but God's love never goes; God will love you forever.

I wonder… is there anything you can do that would make your family or God stop loving you?

6. Moving money wallet

> **You will need: cardboard (an old cereal box is ideal); patterned paper; strips of paper or ribbon (12 cm x 1 cm); tape**

This wallet seemingly moves money from one side to another. Take two pieces of cardboard 10 cm x 7 cm (you could make it slightly larger than your countries paper currency), place them (plain side up if using cereal packets) next to each other in front of you.

Next take two of the strips of paper or ribbon and place them in a narrow or squashed X shape with the centre point in the middle of one of the cardboard rectangles and with all ends extending over the edge of the cardboard. Fold the ends of the paper or ribbon over the edge of one side of the cardboard and secure with tape. Place the second piece of cardboard over the other two ends of the paper. Flip both pieces of card over, and secure the ends of the paper on the back of the second piece of cardboard, then flip back to the front. The strip of paper or ribbon should be an X on one side of the cardboard and the second piece of cardboard should be empty.

Take two more strips of paper or ribbon and place them on the second piece of cardboard, leaving a 0.5 cm gap at the top and bottom, making sure they don't interfere with the X shape. Fold over the outside edge paper ends, then flip over and secure with tape, making sure the two cardboard shapes are level with each other. Flip back to the front, and then tuck the loose edges under the first piece of carboard. Flip over, and secure with tape on the back of the first piece of cardboard.

Use patterned paper to cover the back of the cardboard, hiding the secured ends of paper. Place something representing money under one set of ribbons, either the straight strips or the X, fold the wallet, then re-open it but from the other side. The 'money' will have swapped to the other side.

You can look online for instructions to help.

Talk about the various decisions around money in this parable: the Father's choice to give his son the money; the decisions the son made when spending it; the decisions the friends of the son made as it was being spent and after it was gone; and the older son's reaction when his brother returned home and more gifts were lavished upon him. What decisions do we make as we spend our money?

I wonder... how can you share God's love in your everyday finances?

7. Feed the pig 

You will need: a large cardboard box with a pig head drawn or painted on to it with a wide mouth than has been cut out; plastic sheeting to protect the area; items to be the 'food' to feed the pig (this could be waste food, wet sponges or homemade 'slops')

Sit the pig head on to some plastic sheeting and then aim 'food' into the pig's mouth. You can choose which 'food' you feed your pig, making it as messy as you like. If you choose wet food, you could use spoons to fling the food at the pig, although you may want to protect the area behind and around the pig too.

Talk about how looking after pigs was the worst job that a Jewish man could have, but what could he do? He had no money left and nothing to eat, and he thought he could work his way out of his bad situation.

I wonder... does knowing God loves you make a difference when you are in tricky situations?

8. Home 

You will need: leaves; sticks; twigs; other natural materials

Use sticks to build a shelter for a wild animal. Make the entrance small to keep predators out, use the twigs and leaves to fill in the gaps, to keep the rain out, and add leaves inside for the animal to rest on.

Talk about if you have ever been away from your home and felt home sick. In today's Bible story, the son finally realised that, even as a slave, he would be treated better at home, so he decided to return home.

I wonder... what do you love about your home?

9. How should we love them?

You will need: a large piece of paper or piece of wallpaper; pens for drawing or writing

Draw a large heart on the paper, and in the centre of the heart write: 'We are God's hands and feet.' Encourage people to add people or situations in need of God's love. Then encourage them to either add to any of the situations ways where we as individuals could help or to draw a heart around the situation that they will pray for.

Talk about how there are a lot of mistakes happening in our world. There are a lot of areas where God's love is not seen or felt. How can we help to show God's love?

I wonder... how can you show God's love to your family and friends?

10. Collection box 

You will need: something to collect coins in (e.g. a small empty box, smarties tube or an empty, clean tin can); plain paper; pens

Use the plain paper to cover your tin or box and then using the pens write words or draw pictures of areas of injustice linked with today's Bible story, e.g. cold, hungry, lonely. Then use the box to save loose change and donate this money to a charity that helps people with the concern you have written or drawn about.

Talk about how even today some people do not have enough money for food or a safe place to sleep at night.

I wonder... if you have ever felt really hungry?

Celebration

Gather everyone together and ask if anyone would like to help share the story today. Allocate parts: father, son one, son two, friends, farmer and pigs. Retell this story Jesus told.

The younger son in this story was keen to get his hands on money. Money that he shouldn't have until his father had died. He wanted the money so badly, he asked his dad to give it to him now. His dad gave the money to his younger son, and his son set off on an adventure. The son had lots of money and so he made lots of friends. The son spent the money having fun with all his new friend. Life was good. Life was great. Then there was a famine in the land, and the money ran out. The friends disappeared, and he was alone. Life was not good. Life was bad.

The younger son ended up feeding the pigs at a farm. Those pigs had more to eat than he did. The son's stomach was rumbling (*you could ask half those gathered to make rumbly tummy noises*). His stomach was louder than the pigs grunting (*get the other half of those gathered to imitate the noise that pigs make*). The son was so sad, so lonely and so hungry that he made a decision. He knew his father's servants were treated better than he was being treated now, and so he decided to go home and ask his father to take him back as a servant.

The son's father had been watching for him, every day he looked to see if he could see him coming home. Then one day, he saw a figure. It was a male. It walked like his son. It was his son! The father ran. He picked up the skirts of his robes, and he ran. He ran all the way to greet his son. He hugged him, and he was so pleased to see him. The son was embarrassed. He knew he had done wrong and asked his father to take him back as a servant. The father took him back as a son, putting a ring on his finger and placing a cloak on his shoulders. And he threw a party for him!

The older son was not happy that his younger brother was home. He heard the music from the party and was cross. He said to his father, 'You have never thrown a party for me!' The father replied to his older son, 'You are always with me, and everything I have is yours. But we had to celebrate and be glad, because this brother of yours was dead and is alive again; he was lost and is found.'

I wonder...

- Where is love shown in this parable?
- What is Jesus trying to teach us about God through this parable?
- What does Jesus want us to do with this story?
- Which activity today do you think best fitted with the story?

Prayer

Loving Father God, you love us more than we can ever know or understand. Help us to see your love in the hearts and actions of others and help us shine your love in all we think, say and do. Amen.

Song suggestions

- 'Our God is a great big God'
- 'Jesus loves me, this I know'
- 'All the love in the world' – iSingPOP
- 'Thank you for loving me' – Mark and Helen Johnson (Out of the Ark Music)
- 'Big family of God' – Nick and Becky Drake (Worship for Everyone)

Meal suggestions

Party food, such as hot dogs, party rings, jelly and ice cream.

Session material: March
Integrity: stand up and be counted

by Anne Offler and Sharon Pritchard

Bible story for prep

Daniel 3:13–25 (MSG)

Furious, King Nebuchadnezzar ordered Shadrach, Meshach, and Abednego to be brought in. When the men were brought in, Nebuchadnezzar asked, 'Is it true, Shadrach, Meshach, and Abednego, that you don't respect my gods and refuse to worship the gold statue that I have set up? I'm giving you a second chance – but from now on, when the big band strikes up you must go to your knees and worship the statue I have made. If you don't worship it, you will be pitched into a roaring furnace, no questions asked. Who is the god who can rescue you from my power?'

Shadrach, Meshach, and Abednego answered King Nebuchadnezzar, 'Your threat means nothing to us. If you throw us in the fire, the God we serve can rescue us from your roaring furnace and anything else you might cook up, O king. But even if he doesn't, it wouldn't make a bit of difference, O king. We still wouldn't serve your gods or worship the gold statue you set up.'

Nebuchadnezzar, his face purple with anger, cut off Shadrach, Meshach, and Abednego. He ordered the furnace fired up seven times hotter than usual. He ordered some strong men from the army to tie them up, hands and feet, and throw them into the roaring furnace. Shadrach, Meshach, and Abednego, bound hand and foot, fully dressed from head to toe, were pitched into the roaring fire. Because the king was in such a hurry and the furnace was so hot, flames from the furnace killed the men who carried Shadrach, Meshach, and Abednego to it, while the fire raged around Shadrach, Meshach, and Abednego.

Suddenly King Nebuchadnezzar jumped up in alarm and said, 'Didn't we throw three men, bound hand and foot, into the fire?'

'That's right, O king,' they said.

'But look!' he said. 'I see four men, walking around freely in the fire, completely unharmed! And the fourth man looks like a son of the gods!'

Pointers

- Shadrach, Meshach and Abednego refused to obey the king, as his command was contrary to the command of God to worship only him.
- They stood up for their belief in God even though they might die in the fiery furnace. They were prepared to die rather than worship anything but God.
- Their actions had a profound impact on the king, who recognised their God and respected what they had done.
- They showed integrity in all their decisions.

How does this session help people grow in Christ?

This story shows us that our belief in God can help us to make decisions, even when the decision is a hard one. We can choose what we do and how we respond using all of the things that we have learned about God to help us.

Add value

Mealtime card

- What easy and hard decisions do we make today?
- What do you think Shadrach, Meshach and Abednego thought when told they had to bow to the statue? What would you have thought?
- What things would you stand up for or against today?

Question to start and end the session

So… what would you stand up for based on your faith?

Social action idea

Look for ways to stand up and be counted (e.g. eco-projects, homeless charities, food banks)

Activities

1. It's getting hotter 

You will need: three or four hula hoops with strands of red, yellow or orange ribbon or crepe paper hanging from them; masking tape; chairs; challenge cards printed out

Fasten each hoop between two chairs and line them up to make a tunnel with a challenge card between each. Look ahead at the fiery tunnel. Crawl through the tunnel, stopping and completing each challenge when you see it

Talk about making decisions. Shadrach, Meshach and Abednego made their decision because they believed God was right when he said they should not worship statues. How does God help us to make decisions today?

I wonder… how Shadrach, Meshach and Abednego must have felt as they faced going into the fiery furnace?

2. Foamy flames

You will need: shaving foam; a stirrer; A4 white paper; baking trays or similar; red and yellow paints; a washing line and pegs or similar to dry pictures

Spray shaving foam on to the tray and make it into the shape of a flame with their fingers or the stirrer. Add a few drops of the red and yellow paint and swirl the paint into the foam to make an orangey flame. Lay a piece of paper on to the foam and peel back slowly to reveal the flame painting. Peg it on to the line to dry.

Talk about how the flames in the picture can get bigger when we add more paint or foam. The flames in the furnace also got bigger, but Shadrach, Meshach and Abednego still trusted in God.

I wonder… have you ever been near a fire? What did it feel like?

3. Always with us

You will need: an A4 acetate sheet; battery tealights; yellow, red, orange tissue paper; PVA glue; a spreader; black paper; tape

Cut flames from the tissue paper and stick them to the acetate sheet. Measure a strip of black paper the length of the acetate sheet and about halfway up it. Fold the paper into four in a concertina and then fold it in half. Cut out half of a simple figure ensuring that the main fold is the backbone of the figure and that the arms stay joined. Glue the strip of figures on top of the flames. Keeping the paper to the inside, join the two short ends of the acetate and secure with tape. Put a tealight in the middle of the holder.

Talk about how God is with us always, even when things get difficult. Where was God when Shadrach, Meshach and Abednego were in the fiery furnace? Who was the fourth person?

I wonder… how do we know that God is always with us?

4. Integrity  

You will need: INTEGRITY worksheet printed off for each person or use a scrabble board or other word tile game; pens

Use each letter of the word INTEGRITY to make an acrostic poem or story. An acrostic is when certain letters from a word are used to create other words on the same topic. Think about what integrity means, being honest and keeping to a rule that you do not want to change. You might like to focus your poem on something you believe in strongly.

Talk about when we believe strongly in something right and true, we have integrity. In today's Bible story we learn about three young men who had integrity – and a lot of it! They stood strong and did the right thing, no matter what the circumstances were, not even when they were thrown into a fire-filled furnace! Do you have integrity? Is it easy to have integrity?

I wonder... how difficult was it for Shadrach, Meshach and Abednego to keep their trust in God? How difficult is it for us to keep trusting in God, especially when things are hard?

5. Not three but four

You will need: orange, red and yellow jelly, each colour made up and set in different containers; small gingerbread people shapes, either bought ready or made yourself (recipe in support material section); clear plastic cups; spoons

Remember to risk assess for allergies and intolerances.

Take a cup and put a few spoonfuls of the three coloured jellies into it to resemble fire. Take four gingerbread people and put them in the jelly followed by a few more spoonfuls of the jelly.

Talk about how in our Bible story we learn that there was someone in the fiery furnace with Shadrach, Meshach and Abednego who protected them from the fire.

I wonder... who do you think the fourth person was? Where had they come from and who sent them?

6. Storybox

You will need: a shoebox or similar box filled with items with which to tell the story: e.g. a crown, a gold-covered block with jewel stickers on it, a small musical instrument, four figurines (could be wooden figures, Lego or similar), a paper cup with door cut out and tissue inside to represent flames, rope or cord, flame shapes, a Bible, a small roll of paper tied with ribbon; an abridged copy of the story PDF

Begin to read the story and take out the items to illustrate it. When you have finished, mix up the items on the table. Ask everyone not to look, then take away and cover up one item. Ask everyone to look again and tell you what is missing. Repeat this as often as you choose.

Talk about the different parts of the story. If one part is missing, does it change the story? How?

I wonder... where is God in this story?

7. Flame threading

You will need: white paper plates; pencils; a hole punch; orange wool; brown card; glue or sticky tape

Take the paper plate and draw a flame with the pencil then punch holes in the shape of the flame, with a few holes in a line at the base of the flame. Take long strands of orange wool and thread them though the holes from top to bottom of the flame shape. Cover the base line of holes with two strips of brown card to resemble logs using the glue or sticky tape.

Talk about the different shapes flames can be, always pointing upwards and always moving.

I wonder… what's the bravest thing you've ever done or said as a follower of Jesus?

8. Feel the heat 

You will need: a small fire pit or chimenea; marshmallows; twigs with bark stripped at the top

Set up a small outdoor fire pit, chimenea or fire basket, being mindful of safety and including a fire bucket. Keep people at a safe distance but close enough to be able to see the flames. Ask about the flames, e.g. the different colours or how they move. The burning wood makes smoke – can you smell it? Hold your hands out towards the fire – can you feel the warmth? Put a marshmallow on a stick and toast it – it gets burned. Have a few toasted marshmallows and share them. In our story there was a big tower called a furnace that had fire in it. It would have had flames like our fire, it would have had smoke, and it would have been very hot. When Shadrach, Meshach and Abednego got put into the furnace, they should have been burned – not very nice. But God sent his angel to be with them and protect them. They didn't burn or even smell of smoke – it was an amazing God thing!

Talk about why God did this and why it was something unusual and special.

I wonder… could you say 'no' if you were asked to do something that you knew was wrong?

9. Flame labyrinth  

You will need: a labyrinth in the shape of a flame marked out on the floor, if inside, or on the ground, if in an outdoor space (this can also be done sat around a table, finger walking with individual cards); six small markers or dots placed at intervals in the labyrinth; a set of prayers or prayer topics written on cards (e.g. pray for the world, pray for your community, pray for your friends, pray for your family, pray for yourself, pray as we get closer to the centre of the labyrinth that God will draw close to us)

Walk quietly along the labyrinth stopping at the numbered spots and using the suggested prayer idea on the card.

As an alternative, give people a labyrinth outline on paper. Sit quietly, colouring the flame while thinking about things in our world and community. Draw the labyrinth lines with coloured pens and add numbers to indicate prayer points. Trace around the labyrinth with your finger stopping at the prayer points to pray.

Talk about how our prayers for ourselves and for others bring us closer to God and are part of our faith.

I wonder… what did Shadrach, Meshach and Abednego pray as they were in the furnace? What did they pray when they stepped out of it?

10. Stand up and be counted

You will need: a wooden or card figurine to decorate; collage material (e.g. fabric scraps, wool, lace, coloured pens); glue

Decorate your figure using the materials on the table. When you are finished stand your figure on the table.

Talk about the phrase 'Stand up and be counted'. (Remember it's about standing up in our heart not our body.) What does the phrase mean?

I wonder… what or who can we support locally or in the wider world?

Celebration

Who likes to go to the seaside? Who has bought one of these? (*Hold up a stick of seaside rock. Make sure it has a word running through it.*) What is it? What do you do with it? Have you noticed that it has words on the end of it? Break the rock in two pieces and show that the words run right through it. It's a bit like the jam and cream in a swiss roll. (*Hold up a swiss roll, cut it into pieces or ask for a volunteer to do this and show the jam and cream running all of the way through.*) This helps us to understand our story. Shadrach, Meshach and Abednego wanted to do the things that God had taught them. When they made choices, they always thought about God's teaching. It's like God's teaching was running through them helping them to make good choices. It's something we can do today. When we make choices, we can try to remember what we have learned about Jesus. It's like Jesus is running all the way through us helping us in our choices, our actions, our thoughts. Can anyone tell me what Jesus did? *Expect or prompt to get words like 'kind', 'caring', 'fair', 'honest'.*

I wonder...

- If we can stop and think about Jesus and what he would do in some of the situations we get into?

Prayer

Loving Lord
Thank you for all that you have done
We want to be like you so
Let's stand up and be counted! *Stand up and shout the phrase together.*
When we have difficult decisions to make
Remind us to be like you so
Let's stand up and be counted! *Stand up and shout the phrase together.*
When we see people being treated unfairly
Help us to remember what you would do to put this right so
Let's stand up and be counted! *Stand up and shout the phrase together.*
When we see our world being messed up by the things we do
Help us to find out how we can be more careful so
Let's stand up and be counted! *Stand up and shout the phrase together.*

Song suggestions

- 'Jesus be the centre' – Kathryn Scott and Michael Frye
- 'Be bold, be strong' – Morris Chapman
- 'Great big God' – Jo and Nigel Hemming (Vineyard Kids)
- 'We'll walk with the Lord (Daniel's friends in the fiery furnace)' – DG Bible Songs
- 'Brighter day tomorrow' – Mark and Helen Johnson (Out of the Ark Music)
- 'The rock' – Nick and Becky Drkae (Worship for Everyone)
- 'Say what you mean' – iSingPOP

Meal suggestions

This is a good opportunity to use food that is flame-coloured. Pizzas may be an option with a tomato sauce and cheese, along with a salad containing carrot, red and yellow peppers, sweetcorn and cheese, and sweet potato wedges. Follow with a fruit salad – oranges, peaches, strawberries, pineapple, etc. – along with a slice of the swiss roll used in the celebration talk!

Session material: April
Courage to follow Jesus
by Becky May

Bible story for prep

Luke 19:41 (NIV)

As he approached Jerusalem and saw the city, he wept over it.

Matthew 26:17–29; 36–45 (NIV)

On the first day of the Festival of Unleavened Bread, the disciples came to Jesus and asked, 'Where do you want us to make preparations for you to eat the Passover?'

He replied, 'Go into the city to a certain man and tell him, "The Teacher says: my appointed time is near. I am going to celebrate the Passover with my disciples at your house."' So the disciples did as Jesus had directed them and prepared the Passover.

When evening came, Jesus was reclining at the table with the Twelve. And while they were eating, he said, 'Truly I tell you, one of you will betray me.'

They were very sad and began to say to him one after the other, 'Surely you don't mean me, Lord?'

Jesus replied, 'The one who has dipped his hand into the bowl with me will betray me. The Son of Man will go just as it is written about him. But woe to that man who betrays the Son of Man! It would be better for him if he had not been born.'

Then Judas, the one who would betray him, said, 'Surely you don't mean me, Rabbi?'

Jesus answered, 'You have said so.'

While they were eating, Jesus took bread, and when he had given thanks, he broke it and gave it to his disciples, saying, 'Take and eat; this is my body.'

Then he took a cup, and when he had given thanks, he gave it to them, saying, 'Drink from it, all of you. This is my blood of the covenant, which is poured out for many for the forgiveness of sins. I tell you, I will not drink from this fruit of the vine from now on until that day when I drink it new with you in my Father's kingdom'…

Then Jesus went with his disciples to a place called Gethsemane, and he said to them, 'Sit here while I go over there and pray.' He took Peter and the two sons of Zebedee along with him, and he began to be sorrowful and troubled. Then he said to them, 'My soul is overwhelmed with sorrow to the point of death. Stay here and keep watch with me.'

Going a little farther, he fell with his face to the ground and prayed, 'My Father, if it is possible, may this cup be taken from me. Yet not as I will, but as you will.'

Then he returned to his disciples and found them sleeping. 'Couldn't you men keep watch with me for one hour?' he asked Peter. 'Watch and pray so that you will not fall into temptation. The spirit is willing, but the flesh is weak.'

He went away a second time and prayed, 'My Father, if it is not possible for this cup to be taken away unless I drink it, may your will be done.'

When he came back, he again found them sleeping, because their eyes were heavy. So he left them and went away once more and prayed the third time, saying the same thing.

Then he returned to the disciples and said to them, 'Are you still sleeping and resting? Look, the hour has come, and the Son of Man is delivered into the hands of sinners.'

Pointers

The passages chosen for today's session carry the weight of ominous foreboding. Of course, we know what happens next, how the story continues and even how the story ends; we live as resurrection people.

But these readings, and the opportunity to dwell in these words, bring a different understanding, perhaps. They give us the chance to observe and to walk alongside Jesus as he courageously walks through Holy Week towards the events of Easter. And they give us the opportunity to pause and reflect, to better understand what cost there was to Jesus and how he consciously submitted to this process.

Perhaps this story and these events will become more 'real' for us in taking a slower look at the story, in seeing the emotion Jesus experienced at each stage, from weeping tears to being 'overwhelmed with sorrow to the point of death'. Knowing that Jesus chose to submit to the will of God and 'drink of the cup' reveals something of the courage of Jesus and of the personal cost he endured for us. Above all, for me, it demonstrates what motivated Jesus to go through with this – love.

How does this session help people grow in Christ?

It is the good news revealed in the events of Easter weekend which gives us new life in Jesus. This session takes a look at the steps which lead up to Jesus' death and resurrection and give us all the opportunity to reflect both upon the cost of that new life and what motivated Jesus to go through with it. As we take a slower, more reflective look at the story, we have the opportunity to respond to this for ourselves.

Add value

Mealtime card

- Can you think of a time when you have needed to face something with courage?
- Has this session helped you to see the Easter story differently?
- What questions do you have about this story?

Question to start and end the session

So… why do you think Jesus took this journey?

Social action idea

Why do you think Jesus cried when he looked over the city? Where in your community are people 'crying'? Where might Jesus weep? How can we share God's resurrection hope, in practical ways, in those places?

Activities

1. Walk bravely 

You will need: an obstacle course from different things (e.g. low ropes, sensory materials)

How you choose to organise this activity will depend upon the facilities available to you. You could set up a simple blindfold obstacle course or something more complex, such as a sensory walk or low ropes course. Challenge the participants to be 'brave' and complete the walk.

Talk about how Jesus walked bravely through Holy Week to the events of Easter weekend. Share a personal experience of where you've had to take a 'leap of faith' for Jesus.

I wonder… what gave Jesus the courage to go through with what was needed of him?

2. Make a face 

You will need: mirrors; playdough; a face outline; playdough mats; images of the events of Holy Week and Easter

Share the various pictures of the events of Holy Week and Easter weekend and invite people to think about how Jesus may have felt at each of these moments. Using the mirrors, invite people to pose in an appropriate expression to show this, before creating the same expression with the playdough on the face-shaped mat.

Talk about how Jesus may have felt, introducing the appropriate language to describe the different emotions.

I wonder… how did Jesus feel here (point to each part)? How does this part of the story makes you feel?

3. Form a cross

You will need: wooden bases; nails; hammers; wool or string

You will need to risk assess this activity and ensure that the appropriate safety measures are in place.

You could also provide some bases with nails already in place to give people the choice to create their own base or use one provided. Hammer the nails into the board to form a basic cross template. Provide different coloured lengths of wool or string and invite them to form their cross shape, weaving the wool around the nail structure.

Talk about how and why the cross is significant to us today and what it would have meant to Jesus as he walked though Holy Week.

I wonder... did Jesus think about the cross in that last week? I wonder what he thought?

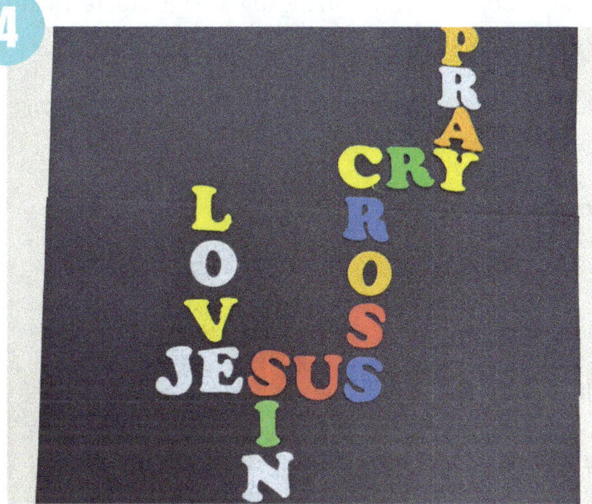

4. Tile by tile

You will need: Scrabble or other letter tiles

Provide a selection of Scrabble tiles and invite participants to form words connected to today's story, added in a 'grid'. This could be done as an individual activity, or collaboratively, with participants each adding and changing words as they come to this activity. Take a photo as a recording of the words formed.

Talk about the different words and why you are choosing to add them. What they mean to you?

I wonder... why is this word important? Which word is the most important?

5. Love is...

You will need: biscuits; love heart sweets; edible pens

Remember to risk assess for allergies and intolerances.

Using the love heart sweets with their many messages as an inspiration, use the biscuits and edible pens to create your own edible love heart messages, based on what we see about Jesus' great act of love. You could use icing to attach a gummy heart to the biscuit or simply draw or write your message.

Talk about what this story shows us about how much God loves us. How can we communicate that?

I wonder... what does this story show about how Jesus loves us?

6. Holy Week wall hanging

You will need: lengths of wide ribbon; Holy Week picture cards (sheets printed on to card); sticky-backed Velcro; colouring pens

Colour and cut out each of the cards for the Holy Week wall hanging. Attach a square of Velcro to the back of each card and its 'partner' on to the ribbon (they should be spread out at regular intervals along the ribbon). Tie a loop at the top of the ribbon so that it can be hung up. When complete, put the hanging up on the wall, and attach the appropriate card on each day of Holy Week.

Talk about what happened on each of these days and why they were important to the story.

I wonder... how did Jesus feel at each stage of this story?

7. Do you dare?

You will need: feely boxes or bags with assorted contents of different textures

Set up a series of simple feely boxes and bags with varied contents, such as a toy spider, cotton wool, cold baked beans, etc. Invite participants to put their hands in and guess what may be hidden within. You could provide a form for them to record their guesses or just invite them to call them out, then reveal the real contents.

Talk about how you felt about putting your hand in. What gave you the courage to do it?

I wonder... what gave Jesus the courage to go through with the events of Easter?

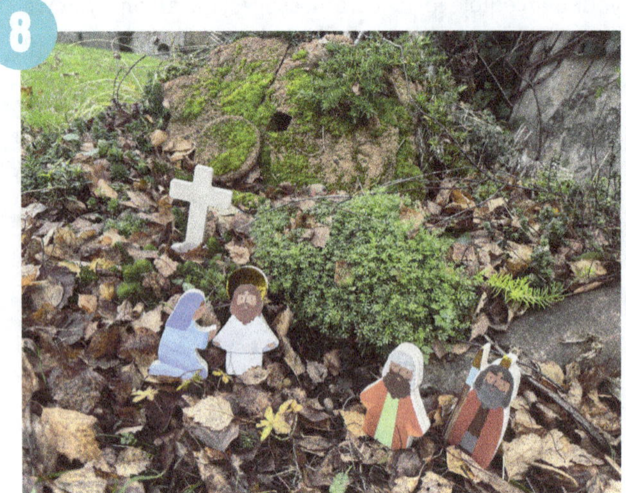

8. Holy Week garden 

You will need: naturally found objects and plants; space outside; props (optional)

It is common for churches to create an 'Easter Garden' with a resurrection theme, but today have a go at creating a Holy Week garden. You could choose to focus on one part of the story (perhaps the garden where Jesus and his disciples went to pray) or the whole story. Use materials already available to you or add in play figures and props which help to tell the story, if you prefer.

Talk about what it would have been like in these places at this time. What would you have seen, heard, smelt?

I wonder… what makes this place so special?

9. Walk and pray 

You will need: access to outside space

Remind your Messy Church that Jesus and his friends went out into the garden that night to pray. Invite participants to take their own short prayer walk in the outdoor space around you. Perhaps you may like to pray together as you walk or find a space where you can be alone to pray, just as Jesus did.

Talk about how Jesus was really honest in his prayer, talking to Father God about how he really felt. Have we ever prayed like that?

I wonder… what might you like to talk to God about today?

10. Love in action 

You will need: magazines and newspapers; scissors; paper; glue; cameras (optional)

Invite participants to look for images of love in action; what does love look like? Invite them to stick them on to the paper to create a collage together. You could create a second collage at the same time entitled 'courage', finding images of what courage may look like. Alternatively, you could do a more 'technical' version of this activity, inviting participants to take their own photos of what 'love' or 'courage' looks like and working together to create a slide show of the images.

Talk about how the different images show love or courage in action.

I wonder… what love looks like?

Celebration

You will need one pipe cleaner for each person. Distribute these before you begin.

I wonder what shape love is. Could you make a shape with your pipe cleaner to show 'love'. You can show us if you like. *Invite people to form their shape and hold them up to show, if they are happy to do so, and take a look at some, commenting on what you have: e.g. 'Oh, we have lots of hearts. Oh, what's that one?'*

As I share our story today, I'm going to show you some of the shapes that God used to show us his love. You can make them with your pipe cleaner if you like.

God loves the world very much (*form a heart*). So much, that God sent his Son, Jesus to earth to be born as a baby on that very first Christmas. When Jesus grew up, he told us more about God's love and showed us too. In his last week on earth, he showed us his love in the greatest way possible.

Sometimes love looks like this (*form a tear shape*). When people we love are hurting, it can make us sad too. *Be careful about the wording here to avoid any suggestion that people who love us should cause us pain!*

Jesus looked out across the city he loved, and he cried. The people God loves so much had walked so far away from him, and Jesus knew he had to do something very courageous to put things right again.

Sometimes love looks like this (*form a table shape*); a meal around a table with family and friends is a great way to share love and spend time with those people who are special to us. Jesus had a special meal with his closest friends. He told them more about what would happen to him, and why he would do this. They didn't really understand at this time, but they would do…

Sometimes love looks like this (*form a flower shape*). People often give flowers to those they love, don't they? After the meal, Jesus went outside into the garden to pray. He needed to be close to Father God and talk to him about what was to happen. Jesus' friends still didn't understand. While Jesus prayed, they fell asleep! I wonder how this made Jesus feel.

Jesus then showed us a different shape that love can take (*form a cross*). The week we have been thinking about today led to this shape – the cross, where Jesus would die. The Bible tells us that this wasn't the end; it was just the beginning! A new beginning! Jesus came back to life again and was reunited with his friends on Easter Day! But this shape is the hardest and the most special. Jesus showed us his love by courageously going to the cross to die for us and make a way for us to be friends with God again.

I wonder...

- Which shape do you think is most important now?
- What does Jesus' love mean to you?

Prayer

Jesus showed us what shape love is. What shape would you like to make to respond to this?

Invite people to form a shape which shows their responses in prayer. You could give a few examples to get people thinking or just give space to create. Invite people to hold up their shapes if they wish or hold it in the palm of their hands as you pray together. Encourage them to take their shape home and put it somewhere as a reminder of their prayer.

Song suggestions

- 'Story of the cross' – Rend Co. Kids
- 'Easter doesn't stop' – Engage Worship
- 'Love, love, love' – Fischy Music
- 'Be strong and courageous' – Doug Horley
- 'He is risen (Easter blessing)' – Mark and Helen Johnson (Out of the Ark Music)
- 'Sign your cross' – Nick and Becky Drake (Worship for Everyone)
- 'Fighting for love' – iSingPOP

Meal suggestions

Baguette pizzas with toppings, followed by seasonally decorated chocolate cake (and a fruit alternative!)

Session material: May
Community: a home for all
by the Messy Church Conference 2025 planning team

 **SUPPORT MATERIAL**    **MESSY CHURCH AT HOME**    **MESSY CHURCH GOES WILD**

Bible story for prep

1 Corinthians 12:12–27 (MSG)

You can easily enough see how this kind of thing works by looking no further than your own body. Your body has many parts – limbs, organs, cells – but no matter how many parts you can name, you're still one body. It's exactly the same with Christ. By means of his one Spirit, we all said good-bye to our partial and piecemeal lives. We each used to independently call our own shots, but then we entered into a large and integrated life in which *he* has the final say in everything. (This is what we proclaimed in word and action when we were baptised.) Each of us is now a part of his resurrection body, refreshed and sustained at one fountain – his Spirit – where we all come to drink. The old labels we once used to identify ourselves – labels like Jew or Greek, slave or free – are no longer useful. We need something larger, more comprehensive.

I want you to think about how all this makes you more significant, not less. A body isn't just a single part blown up into something huge. It's all the different-but-similar parts arranged and functioning together. If Foot said, 'I'm not elegant like Hand, embellished with rings; I guess I don't belong to this body,' would that make it so? If Ear said, 'I'm not beautiful like Eye, transparent and expressive; I don't deserve a place on the head,' would you want to remove it from the body? If the body was all eye, how could it hear? If all ear, how could it smell? As it is, we see that God has carefully placed each part of the body right where he wanted it.

But I also want you to think about how this keeps your significance from getting blown up into self-importance. For no matter how significant you are, it is only because of what you are a *part* of. An enormous eye or a gigantic hand wouldn't be a body, but a monster. What we have is one body with many parts, each its proper size and in its proper place. No part is important on its own. Can you imagine Eye telling Hand, 'Get lost; I don't need you'? Or, Head telling Foot, 'You're fired; your job has been phased out'? As a matter of fact, in practice it works the other way – the 'lower' the part, the more basic, and therefore necessary. You can live without an eye, for instance, but not without a stomach. When it's a part of your own body you are concerned with, it makes *no* difference whether the part is visible or clothed, higher or lower. You give it dignity and honour just as it is, without comparisons. If anything, you have more concern for the lower parts than the higher. If you had to choose, wouldn't you prefer good digestion to full-bodied hair?

The way God designed our bodies is a model for understanding our lives together as a church: every part dependent on every other part, the parts we mention and the parts we don't, the parts we see and the parts we don't. If one part hurts, every other part is involved in the hurt, and in the healing. If one part flourishes, every other part enters into the exuberance.

You are Christ's body – that's who you are! You must never forget this.

Pointers

The apostle Paul uses the image of a human body more than once in his letters to help his readers understand how the church should work. Our bodies are made up of many different parts, each with their own particular functions and vital contribution to the overall health of a person. Some of these parts are very visible and, superficially at least, seem to be more significant, but in fact our hidden organs and blood vessels beneath the skin are just as important, if not more so. Paul transfers these ideas to illustrate how every single person is important and has a part to play in making Christ known.

How does this session help people grow in Christ?

- We sometimes forget that Paul's letters to the churches in places like Rome, Philippi and Corinth were read out to the whole gathered congregation. These weren't private, specialist communications to particular leaders or age groups in those churches. Everyone heard what Paul had to say, and they understood that his words were for everyone – including household slaves, women, children and even some of 'the outsiders' who were perhaps 'just looking' when it came to the matter of faith in Jesus.

- When we hear what Paul has to say about the church being the body of Christ, any of those listening might well be the hand, foot, eyes or ears that he is talking about. There is no sense here that only those who have reached a certain level of spiritual maturity are qualified to be particular limbs. In fact, the whole thrust of what Paul is saying is that some of the least likely members of a congregation may well be the most significant parts of Christ's body, the church.

- Messy Church fully embraces this idea of 'every-member ministry', with its emphasis on the importance of team leadership and the valuing of young and old in the togetherness that makes this fresh expression of church possible.

Add value

Mealtime card

- Food helps fuel our physical bodies. What helps fuel the body of Christ?

- What have you heard today that has challenged you?

- What have you seen today that has made you joyful?

Question to start and end the session

So… have you ever thought that the church is like a body with lots of different parts?

Social action idea

Before the next Messy Church, challenge your family to find ways of using their hands, feet, eyes, ears and mouths to be the body of Christ at home, at school, at work or in your neighbourhood. Each day, focus on one of these parts of the body and work out something good that you could do, which would please God and be a blessing to others. For example, hands could carry something for a person who is struggling; feet could go on an errand for someone who can't.

Activities

1. Different body parts working together 

You will need: blindfolds; bands/scarfs

Have a three-legged race! If you want to make it more challenging, one of the team could be blindfolded.

Talk about how it felt when you weren't allowed to use one part of your body. Was it easier or harder than you were expecting?

I wonder… what holds you back from sharing the good news of Jesus in your everyday life?

2. Design a church

You will need: either sweets and cocktail sticks or marshmallows and spaghetti, or Lego/Duplo

Design a church using the modelling materials – not a building necessarily, but what a church could be. How big can you make it? How connected can you make it?

Talk about if everyone is making separate models or one all together. Are they better apart or together? What holds the church together? What breaks it up?

I wonder… what is the most important aspect of a church, as far as you're concerned?

3. The everybody challenge

You will need: cardboard; plastic balls or small bean bags; scissors

Cut out a large body shape from a big piece of cardboard and mount it so that it can stand upright. Cut holes in the cardboard at the mouth, hands, knees, heart and waist.

Challenge everyone to see how many bean bags or balls they can get through the holes in the body within a certain time limit and from an agreed distance.

Talk about which parts of the body of Christ you think might be missing at this Messy Church.

I wonder… how does it feel when there are parts (people) missing?

4. Body prayers 

You will need: card or paper people outlines; crayons or felt-tip pens

Use the crayons or felt-tip pens to decorate the people outlines with your gifts or talents.

Talk about how the Bible passage is also about gifts that we bring to the body. Give thanks for the gifts we have and pray for gifts that are missing from our Messy Church.

I wonder… how could you use the gifts you have been given to help share the good news about Jesus?

5. Rainbow people

You will need: ready-made gingerbread people; icing; food colouring

Decorate each section of a gingerbread person in a different colour.

Talk about how 'God's rainbow people' could well be a description for the church, with each person contributing their own special colour to the overall body of Christ.

I wonder… in what ways is your Messy Church a rainbow of different people?

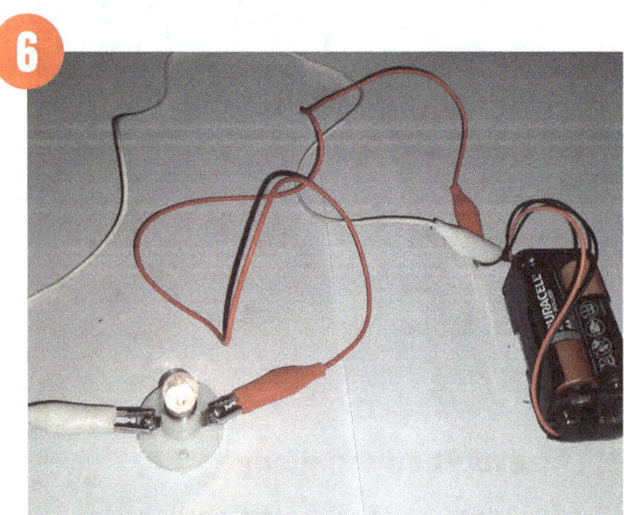

6. Making connections

You will need: equipment to make a simple electrical circuit (leads, crocodile clips, a bulb, a battery)

Connect the different components to make a simple electrical circuit and see if you can make the bulb light up. You can find simple instructions to follow on various websites.

Talk about how all the parts of the circuit are very different but without them all being connected you can't make the circuit complete. If our churches are missing one part then people may not be able to see the light.

I wonder… what happens if you take away one part of the electrical circuit?

7. Body art 

You will need: paper; paint; soap; water

Make pieces of artwork using your hands/feet/nose/any other body part you don't mind getting paint on!

Talk about how it felt using different body parts to paint with rather than using a paint brush. Did you create something that you wouldn't otherwise have made? Was it messier than your usual artwork?

I wonder… do you think some people can be more than one part of the body of the church?

8. Skeleton bodies 

You will need: either 1) packets of broad craft sticks, a sharp implement to make holes, split pin fasteners; or 2) a variety of pasta shapes, PVA glue, card

Prepare the craft sticks beforehand by making a hole at each end. Invite people to design their own skeleton bodies with the craft sticks and pin all the parts together so they become jointed and movable. Or use the pasta and glue to create a skeleton on the card.

You could make this an outdoor activity by scavenging items from nature to make a body.

Talk about how Teresa of Ávila famously said that 'Christ has no body now but ours, no hands and feet but ours'. Each one of us is part of Christ's body, and each of us can be the hands and feet of Jesus for others.

I wonder… which part of a church is like the hands of Jesus? Which part is like the feet?

9. Pebble prayers 

You will need: a collection of pebbles; permanent markers

Write your name on a pebble. See if you can form the shape of a body with all the pebbles. Each person can take home a pebble with another's name on and pray for them.

Talk about how we are all unique parts of the body of Christ, just as each pebble is unique and different.

I wonder… how does it feel to see your pebble as part of the larger body?

10. The church is the people

You will need: a large sheet of paper or lining paper; creative materials like pens, pencils, stickers, tissue paper, etc.

Draw a large outline of a church building on lining paper. Fill with a visual representation of everyone at your Messy Church. You could use your cut-out people shapes, painted handprints/footprints, or draw your own self-portrait.

Talk about how the church can still be the church when we aren't gathered together.

I wonder… what would it be like if we tried to be church even when we are not all gathered together?

Celebration

Gather everyone for the celebration, using some appropriate music for this occasion, such as Fischy Music's 'Everybody's body' song. Welcome everyone and use the various activities to help set the scene for the story.

Introduce the Bible story today with the song 'Head, shoulders, knees and toes'. Touch each part of the body as you prepare, then sing. You can develop this nursery song further by leaving out some words each time and just touching the part of the body instead, until finally it is an almost silent song, just with the word 'and' every now and then.

That was a song all about the body – the church is like a body! It's made up of many people who are the body's many parts. In the Bible, the writer Paul describes a church as a human body with different parts – and every part is important. Listen to this story that Paul told about the church being the body of Christ.

Divide your Messy congregation into two. Invite everyone to stand and wiggle different parts of the body – hands, head, feet, toes and so on.

The body of Christ has many parts, just like our human bodies. It's not just one part that's all the same, but it is made up of many parts that are all different.

Ask one half of the congregation to wave a foot, and the other half to wave a hand.

A foot can't say, 'I'm not a hand, so I don't belong to the body.' And a hand can't say, 'I'm not a foot, so I don't belong to the body.'

Ask one half to hold on to both ears, and the other half to point to both eyes and blink a lot.

The ears can't say, 'I'm not an eye, so I don't belong to the body.' The eyes can't say, 'I'm not an ear, so I don't belong to the body.' If our bodies were only eyes, then we couldn't hear or eat or run. If our bodies were only ears, then we couldn't smell or see or taste. God has put all the parts of the body together in the best possible way, so each part has a role to play. It is the same with the church, which is Christ's body on earth. Everyone in it has a part to play.

Ask everyone to 'hide' their hands up their sleeves or behind their backs.

Our eyes can't do without our hands. How would we pick up what they see?

Ask everyone to kneel on the ground to hide their feet.

Our hands can't do without our feet. How would they reach what they want to pick up?

Ask everyone to look embarrassed and coy.

Some of the less beautiful parts of the body are the most important… just imagine not having a bottom!

Invite everyone to stand up and wave everything.

God has put together the body so that every part needs every other part. All the parts are valuable and important.

Invite everyone to hold their head as if they have a headache.

If one part of the body hurts, it affects the whole body.

Invite everyone to do some star jumps.

What's good for one part of the body is good for the whole body. It's the same with us in the church. Each one can be part of Christ's body and each one has a vital part to play.

Clear a space in the middle of your congregation, or invite everyone to move to a nearby open area.

Let's draw a huge body on the ground. Then let's all come and stand on the part of that imagined body where we think we might be in the body of the church.

I wonder...

- Which part of the body are you or could you be?
- What are you good at? Is it listening or speaking? Is it seeing what needs to be done or helping others? Is it doing something that no one else notices?

Prayer

Invite people to touch the following body parts as you pray.

Head: Thank you, caring God, for people with gifts of planning and organising.

Shoulders: Thank you, loving God, for people with gifts of taking responsibility and bearing other people's burdens.

Knees: Thank you, awesome God, for people with the gifts of praying and getting down on their knees to play with children.

Toes: Thank you, God of new beginnings, for people with the gifts of getting things started, being pioneers, pushing the church off on a journey of mission and helping it keep a balance between mission and ministry.

Eyes: Thank you, all-seeing God, for people with the gifts of seeing what needs to be done and spotting those who are new and feeling lost.

Ears: Thank you, all-knowing God, for people with the gifts of listening to what people are really saying and hearing what is not said.

Mouth: Thank you, hopeful God, for people with the gifts of telling stories and knowing the right things to say to make visitors feel welcomed and loved.

Nose: Thank you, generous God, for people with the gifts of creating tasty and appetising food that smells mouth-wateringly good.

Thank you, almighty God, for giving each of us gifts to bless others in our churches, in our communities and in our world. We are the body of Christ and individually members of it; we are all needed to be his hands and feet in this world. Amen.

End with the Messy Grace: May the grace of the Lord Jesus Christ, and the love of God and the fellowship of the Holy Spirit be with us all, now and evermore. Amen.

Song suggestions

- 'Everybody's body' – Fischy Music
- 'The body song' – Sam Hargreaves
- 'All are welcome' – Marty Haugen
- 'We're not alone' – iSingPOP
- 'Parts of a body' – Mark and Helen Johnson (Out of the Ark Music)
- 'The golden rule' – Nick and Becky Drake (Worship for Everyone)

Meal suggestions

Sausages and mash, followed by the gingerbread people made during the activities.

This session has been adapted from Martyn Payne's *Messy Togetherness,* a second edition of which was published by BRF Ministries in May 2025.

Session material: June
Purpose: what am I to do?
By Helen Laird

Bible story for prep

Exodus 3 (ICB)

One day Moses was taking care of Jethro's sheep. Jethro was the priest of Midian and also Moses' father-in-law. Moses led the sheep to the west side of the desert. He came to Sinai, the mountain of God. There the angel of the Lord appeared to Moses in flames of fire coming out of a bush. Moses saw that the bush was on fire, but it was not burning up. So Moses said, 'I will go closer to this strange thing. How can a bush continue burning without burning up?'

The Lord saw Moses was coming to look at the bush. So God called to him from the bush, 'Moses, Moses!'

And Moses said, 'Here I am.'

Then God said, 'Do not come any closer. Take off your sandals. You are standing on holy ground. I am the God of your ancestors. I am the God of Abraham, the God of Isaac and the God of Jacob.' Moses covered his face because he was afraid to look at God.

The Lord said, 'I have seen the troubles my people have suffered in Egypt. And I have heard their cries when the Egyptian slave masters hurt them. I am concerned about their pain. I have come down to save them from the Egyptians. I will bring them out of that land. I will lead them to a good land with lots of room. This is a land where much food grows. This is the land of these people: the Canaanites, Hittites, Amorites, Perizzites, Hivites and Jebusites. I have heard the cries of the people of Israel. I have seen the way the Egyptians have made life hard for them. So now I am sending you to the king of Egypt. Go! Bring my people, the Israelites, out of Egypt!'

But Moses said to God, 'I am not a great man! Why should I be the one to go to the king and lead the Israelites out of Egypt?'

God said, 'I will be with you. This will be the proof that I am sending you: You will lead the people out of Egypt. Then all of you will worship me on this mountain.'

Moses said to God, 'When I go to the Israelites, I will say to them, 'The God of your ancestors sent me to you.' What if the people say, "What is his name?" What should I tell them?'

Then God said to Moses, 'I AM WHO I AM. When you go to the people of Israel, tell them, "I AM sent me to you."'

God also said to Moses, 'This is what you should tell the people: "The Lord is the God of your ancestors. He is the God of Abraham, the God of Isaac and the God of Jacob. And he sent me to you." This will always be my name. That is how people from now on will know me.

'Go and gather the elders and tell them this: "The Lord, the God of your ancestors, has appeared to me. The God of Abraham, Isaac and Jacob spoke to me. He says: I care about you, and I have seen what has happened to you in Egypt. I have decided that I will take you away from the troubles you are suffering in Egypt. I will lead you to the land of the Canaanites, Hittites, Amorites, Perizzites, Hivites and Jebusites. This land grows much food."

'The elders will listen to you. And then you and the elders of Israel will go to the king of Egypt. You will tell him, "The Lord, the God of the Hebrews, appeared to us. Let us travel three days into the desert. There we must offer sacrifices to the Lord our God."

'But I know that the king of Egypt will not let you go. Only a great power will force him to let you go. So I will use my great power against Egypt. I will make miracles happen in that land. After I do this, he will let you go. And I will cause the Egyptian people to think well of the people of Israel. So when you leave, they will give gifts to your people… You will put those gifts on your children when you leave Egypt. In this way you will take with you the riches of the Egyptians.'

Pointers

God can use us, no matter how old we are. We can share Jesus' love by being loving or point to Jesus through the way we live our lives. In his old age, Moses was specially selected by God to do an important task. God has a purpose for us all. God used a burning bush to get Moses' attention so that he would hear what God had in mind. How will God share his purpose for you to you?

How does this session help people grow in Christ?

- The session helps us all to see that God is active in our lives and will use us to further God's kingdom if we are ready and willing.

Add value

Mealtime card

- Have you ever received a message you felt was from God?
- I wonder what God's purpose is for you?
- Which of your gifts and skills do you think God might use?

Question to start and end the session

So… Moses was quite old when he saw the burning bush. What do you think he felt and thought? What ways might God use you?

Social action idea

Sell cakes to raise money for Amnesty International or another charity important to your Messy Church.

Activities

1. Shining the light

You will need: a large piece of black cardboard or cardboard painted black (with sections cut out like a stained-glass window); tissue paper; glue; tape

Use tissue paper to fill the spaces to design a stained-glass window.

Talk about how God used a bright flame in a burning bush to get the attention of Moses. God gave Moses a task and then Moses shined the love of God to a whole nation.

I wonder… how do you shine God's love for others to see?

2. Burning bush

You will need: the PDF template; green pencils or crayons; yellow and orange paint

Use the green pencils/crayons to add leaves and then the paint to add flames to the bush template.

Talk about how brave Moses must have been to go near the bush. Share a personal example of when you've felt prompted by God to step outside your comfort zone.

I wonder… what did Moses think when he saw a bush on fire but not burning away?

3. Signpost

You will need: plain fabric material pieces (approximately 25 x 10 cm); needles; thread; a pencil

Encourage those taking part to write 'Purpose' on their sign in pencil. Use the needle and thread to pick out the letters, using a running stitch, small crosses or stitch of their choice.

Talk about how we all have a purpose whether young or old, which may change over time. This sign will be a reminder to always be ready to hear God's purpose for you or for others. Place it somewhere that will catch your eye and encourage you to keep listening to God.

I wonder… have you ever received a sign from God?

4. God's app 

You will need: pens; paper

Create a message from God as if you've just received it on your phone or a messaging app.

Talk about how you prefer to receive messages (phone, text, letter, etc.)? God used a burning bush to get the attention of Moses and give him a specific task. God has a purpose for you – what talents, gifts or skills could God use?

I wonder… how do you listen to God? What might God be asking us to do? What's our purpose?

5. Edible burning bush 

You will need: carrots; red/orange peppers; breadsticks; marmite and/or humous; paper cake cases; pens

Remember to risk assess for allergies and intolerances.

Encourage those taking part to add their name to the underside of a paper cake case, then to create a burning bush, using the breadsticks as wood, the vegetables as flames and the marmite or humous as edible glue.

Talk about how Moses had an important task to do for God, a task that probably felt impossible. I wonder if that is why God got Moses' attention in such a spectacular way? A burning bush that doesn't burn seems impossible to us, but it got Moses' attention.

I wonder… how do you think Moses felt hearing the voice of God and being asked to do such a difficult task? Have you ever been asked to do a difficult task? What was it and how did that feel?

6. The very air we breathe

You will need: tealight candles; glass jars of various sizes; matches; a timer

Light a tealight candle and place a jam jar over it. Time how long it takes for the candle to go out. Experiment with the different sized jars.

Talk about how God provides the very air we breathe. Any flame requires oxygen (found in air) to be able to burn. Without it the flame goes out. Oxygen has a purpose; it keeps a flame going.

I wonder… what kept Moses going as he carried out God's purpose? What keeps you going? How do you connect with God?

7. I AM 

You will need: whatever material you can find outside (e.g. grass, sticks, weeds, mud)

Find a way in your space to write the words 'I AM'.

Talk about when Moses heard God calling him, he replied, 'Here I am.' When Moses asked what God should be called God said, 'I AM WHO I AM. This is what you are to say to the Israelites: "I AM has sent me to you."' This is God telling his people his name. Discuss names and how important they are.

I wonder… what does your name mean?

8. Fat ball 

You will need: paper cups; string; fat (such as lard or suet); bird seed; dried fruit; empty clean yoghurt pots or similar; bradawl; a hammer

Prepare the feeder. Use the bradawl and hammer to put a small hole in the bottom of your pot. Create a circle of string by knotting two ends together; the knot needs to be bigger than the hole in your pot. Pass the string through the hole, leaving the knot on the inside, you could add a disc of paper into the pot at this stage to help seal the hole.

Make the fat ball. The mix requires one part fat to two parts food. Warm the fat on a camping stove, when it has melted add your chosen selection of dried food. Mix well, and then add to your pot and allow to set.

Once set, hang it in the garden.

Talk about how Moses was looking after sheep when God asked him to do a special job. We can't all look after sheep, but in this activity we are going to look after birds. God asked everyone to take care of the creatures of the earth. Feeding the birds is one way we can do that.

I wonder… do you look after any animals? I wonder how many birds will come to your feeder?

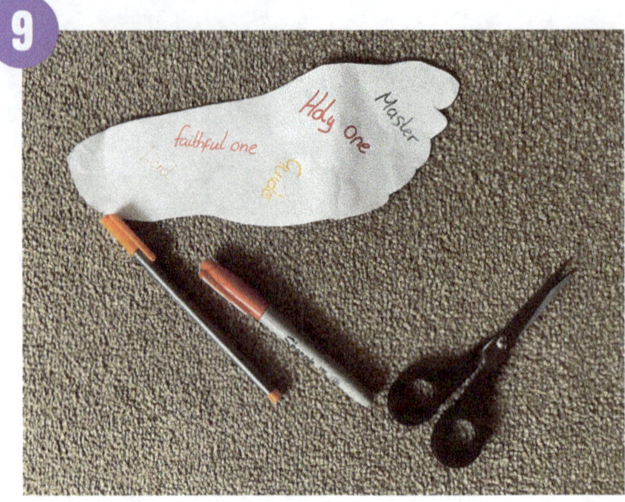

9. This is holy ground 

You will need: paper; scissors; pens; a lamp/ large candle

Remove your shoes, draw around your foot on the paper, then cut out the shape of your foot. Now write a prayer or words of praise and thanksgiving on your foot shape, and place them near the lamp. Ask that God uses you and lights your way.

Talk about how Moses had to remove his shoes, as he was standing on holy ground. Even though Moses was getting old in years, God still used him. God can use us too, but we need to be listening for God's call to us.

I wonder… what is God's purpose for you during this season of life?

10. Take action 

You will need: a laptop or phone connected to the internet

Look at **amnesty.org/en/get-involved/take-action,** select an initiative you would like to support and sign your name to their appeal document.

Talk about how the task God had for Moses was to free the Israelites from their captivity by the Egyptians. Amnesty International is a worldwide organisation that helps to make the world a fairer place. Their website states: 'Amnesty supporters are making the world a fairer place. Because of the actions of individuals, lives have been saved, unfair laws have changed, the wrongfully imprisoned have been released. Your actions make a difference.'

I wonder… how will your actions today make a difference?

Celebration

Have a model of a burning bush, lamp or cross as a focal point to this session. Act out the story. You will need a narrator, Moses, God and sheep. The below language is based off the NIV.

Narrator   Moses was tending the flock of Jethro his father-in-law. He led them to the far side of the wilderness and came to Horeb, the mountain of God. An angel of the Lord appeared to him in flames of fire from within a bush. Moses saw that, though the bush was on fire, it did not burn. Moses went up to the bush.

Moses   Look at this strange sight – why the bush does not burn up?

God   Moses! Moses!

Moses   Here I am.

God   Do not come any closer, take off your sandals, for the place where you are standing is holy ground. I am the God of your father, the God of Abraham, the God of Isaac and the God of Jacob.

Moses hides his face and takes his shoes off.

God   I have seen the misery of my people in Egypt. I have heard them crying out because of their slave drivers, and I am concerned about their suffering. I have come down to rescue them from the hand of the Egyptians and to bring them up out of that land into a good and spacious land, a land flowing with milk and honey. I am sending you to the king of Egypt to bring my people the Israelites out of Egypt.

Moses   Who am I that I should go to the king of Egypt and bring the Israelites out of Egypt?

God   I will be with you. And this will be the sign to you that it is I who have sent you: When you have brought the people out of Egypt, you will worship God on this mountain.

Moses   Suppose I go to the Israelites and say to them, 'The God of your fathers has sent me to you,' and they ask me, 'What is his name?' Then what shall I tell them?

God   I AM WHO I AM. This is what you are to say to the Israelites: 'I AM has sent me to you.' Say to the Israelites, 'The Lord, the God of your fathers – the God of Abraham, the God of Isaac and the God of Jacob – has sent me to you.' This is my name forever, the name you shall call me from generation to generation. Go, assemble the elders of Israel and say to them, 'The Lord, the God of your fathers – the God of Abraham, Isaac and Jacob – appeared to me and said: I have watched over you and have seen what has been done to you in Egypt. And I have promised to bring you up out of your misery in Egypt into the land flowing with milk and honey.'

I wonder...

- What do you think Moses thought when he was given the task?
- How do you think the elders of Israel felt when Moses told them?
- What would the king of Egypt say?

Prayer

Dear I AM, we come before you now, seeking your purpose and clarity for our lives. We ask that we are filled with wisdom and understanding so that we may know the direction in which you want us to go. Amen.

Song suggestions

- 'Oceans' – Hillsong United
- 'What a beautiful name' – Hillsong
- 'Our God is a great big God' – Vineyard
- 'My God is so big' – Cedarmont Kids
- 'Praise to the one' – Mark and Helen Johnson (Out of the Ark Music)
- 'Lighting up the world' – iSingPOP
- 'Every step' – Nick and Becky Drake (Worship for Everyone)

Meal suggestions

Casserole cooked with red, yellow and orange peppers or, to link with the 'land of milk and honey', make honey sandwiches. Pudding could be smores: melt a marshmallow over a tealight flame, then sandwich it between two chocolate biscuits. Or to link with the 'land of milk and honey', rice pudding or similar.

Session material: July
Justice

by Dawn Savidge

Bible story for prep

Luke 4:16–21 (NLT)

When he came to the village of Nazareth, his boyhood home, he went as usual to the synagogue on the Sabbath and stood up to read the Scriptures. The scroll of Isaiah the prophet was handed to him. He unrolled the scroll and found the place where this was written:

'The Spirit of the Lord is upon me, for he has anointed me to bring Good News to the poor. He has sent me to proclaim that captives will be released, that the blind will see, that the oppressed will be set free, and that the time of the Lord's favour has come.'

He rolled up the scroll, handed it back to the attendant, and sat down. All eyes in the synagogue looked at him intently. Then he began to speak to them. 'The Scripture you've just heard has been fulfilled this very day!'

Matthew 5:13–16 (NLT)

'You are the salt of the earth. But what good is salt if it has lost its flavour? Can you make it salty again? It will be thrown out and trampled underfoot as worthless.

'You are the light of the world – like a city on a hilltop that cannot be hidden. No one lights a lamp and then puts it under a basket. Instead, a lamp is placed on a stand, where it gives light to everyone in the house. In the same way, let your good deeds shine out for all to see, so that everyone will praise your heavenly Father.'

Pointers

- Luke recalls Jesus' first time reading in the synagogue, where they would read from the law and from one of the prophets. Jesus reads part of Isaiah 61 and then states that the scripture had now been fulfilled. This was shocking to the people there, as Jesus claimed to be a royal figure and to have a prophetic mission; that he would proclaim freedom to the prisoners; proclaim good news to the poor; recover sight for the blind; set the oppressed free; forgive debts and set slaves free (year of the Lord's favour). Jesus was stating that the 'me' was him.

- The reading in Matthew is taken from the middle of the sermon on the mount. Jesus sets out how we can carry out the work that God has given us to do. We are to be salt and light in the world by telling people about Jesus. Having a relationship with Jesus enables us to be free, which is what Jesus stated his mission was in Luke.

- Salt was used as a preservative for food. It would slow down the deterioration process. In the same way, we are not to lose our saltness and become useless to the world.

- Light is used to dispel darkness. Christians do not have inherent light, but rather we have reflective light. In other words, we reflect what is inside us, and that is Jesus.

- To be both salty and light-bearers, we must ensure that we are filled with God's word and love.

How does this session help people grow in Christ?

- As Christians, we are called to be in the world but not of the world (John 17:14–15). This means that instead of living in a 'bubble', we should recognise injustices in the world, such as poverty, discrimination, the refugee crisis, slavery, etc. And by being Jesus' light and salt in the world, we should be able to be an ambassador for Christ, representing his kingdom to those who do not yet know him.

- This session allows your Messy Church family to look at some of the injustices in the world and in your locality and think about different ways they can be salt and light.

Add value

Mealtime card

- What is one unfairness that you really don't like?
- Tell me about one kind thing you did this week.
- What has been your favourite activity today and why?

Question to start and end the session

So… Jesus came to earth to free people from hurt and he has asked us to carry on doing this with him. He asks us to be salt and light in the world. Are you up for the challenge?

Social action idea

Find ways to give light to your community. It could be visiting an old people's home, starting a choir of hope or even offering to clean cars. Try to think up some random acts of kindness with your Messy Church family.

Activities

1. Ice challenge

You will need: ice cubes; glasses filled with water; string; fine salt

This is a challenge activity which involves seeing whether people can move the ice cubes from one glass to the next without getting their hands wet and using only the string! Let them try to move it with just the string (no flicking of ice cubes allowed). The answer is to put salt on the strong, then put the string around the ice cube. As the salt touches the ice, it will melt and should create enough 'hold' to transfer the ice to the other glass.

Talk about what difference the salt made to the challenge. What difference should we make in the world?

I wonder… what is salt used for? And what did Jesus mean by us being salt in the world?

2. Suncatcher

You will need: tissue paper; greaseproof paper; lollipop sticks; PVA glue; string

Tear up different sizes of coloured tissue paper. Cut up the greaseproof paper into squares (30 cm x 30 cm is a good size). Glue the surface of the greaseproof paper. Stick the tissue paper across the square. When finished, add a lollipop stick frame. Add a piece of string to the top so that it can be hung from a window.

Talk about how a suncatcher catches the light and it looks beautiful. What ways can we be 'suncatchers' (e.g. smile, say hello)?

I wonder… what will happen when the sunshine comes through the window and shines through your suncatcher?

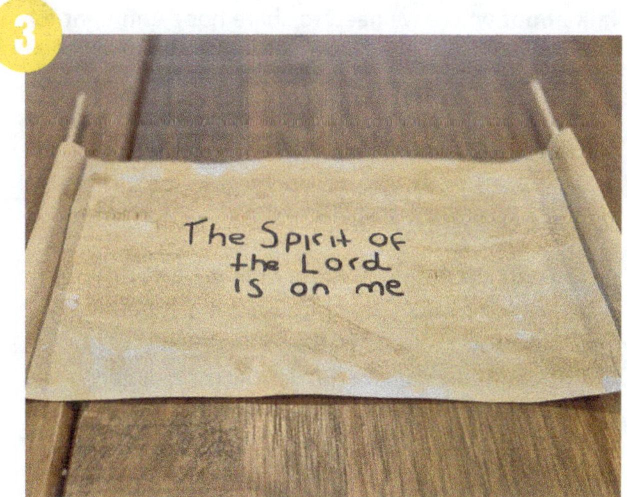

3. A step in the past

You will need: long rolls of paper; a pot of tea with teabags in and left to go cold; cotton wool; rounded skewers; black pens or felt-tips; copies of Luke 4:18–19; a hairdryer; pieces of ribbon

Make an ancient scroll like the one that Jesus read from. Get a long piece of paper. Dip cotton wool in the cold tea and use it to stain the paper. Carefully use a hairdryer to dry the paper – it should curl up as it dries quickly (moving the hairdryer about the paper is the safest way to dry it). Once dried, glue two skewers either side of the long paper. Write out the Bible verses on your scroll. Roll the scroll up and use the ribbon to tie it closed.

Talk about the importance of words. What does the Bible reading mean?

I wonder... why were the people in the synagogue mad when Jesus read the scriptures? What words have made you angry lately and why?

4. Letter of hope 

You will need: writing paper; envelopes; pens; blank cards to write in

This is a chance to do one of two things. Firstly, you could get some of the older Messy Church family members to write a letter to an MP about a local or national issue that needs God's light shining in on. Secondly, you could get the younger Messy Church family members to make a card of hope for a friend, local charity or local old people's home, being the light in a dark place.

This is a free activity but print out some ideas to help encourage creativity. For example, where are the local charities or old people's homes? What are the local and national issues that Parliament needs to know about. Look at places like Christian Concern or your local pages on social media for ideas.

Talk about where we need to share hope and fight for justice.

I wonder... why have people lost hope and where can we shine light?

5. Ice cream in a bag

You will need: milk (whole milk is best) or alternative milk (soya, almond, etc.); plastic ziplock food bags (small and large); ice; fine salt; vanilla essence (for flavouring); sugar; tea towels

Pour a glass of milk, 1 tablespoon of sugar and ½ teaspoon of vanilla essence into a ziplock bag and fasten it tightly, making sure you get any excess air out. In a larger ziplock bag, fill it half full of ice and add ¼ cup of salt. Put the smaller bag of milk inside the big bag of ice. Fasten the big bag. Using a tea towel (to prevent your hands from getting cold), shake the bag. After about five minutes take the small milk bag out; you should now have a bag of ice cream. If it looks icy, use a spoon to stir it and it should soften up.

Talk about how this experiment works. It's an exothermic reaction, meaning that the chemical reaction releases light/heat. In this case, heat is released from molecules moving around, freezing the milk into ice-cream. Salt lowers the melting temperature of the ice, so that it stays colder for longer, freezing the milk faster.

I wonder... why do we need salt for this to work? What difference can we make by being 'salt' in the world.

6. Lava lamp

You will need: vegetable oil; water; salt; food colouring; glasses or containers with lids

Pour 240 ml of water into a container. If you are adding food colouring, do this now. Add 80 ml of oil on top. Let it settle. Sprinkle salt over the top, a teaspoon at a time. Watch the bubbles form. Try mixing up the oil and water and see what happens.

Talk about how Jesus calls us to be salt and light in the world. This means being different and showing God's love but also calling out when we see injustices. The jar represents the world. The water represents those who don't yet know Jesus. We are the oil; we sit in the world but are called to be different from the world. When we are like salt in the world, we become like the bubbles around those people who don't yet know who Jesus is. We share Jesus' love for people and justice in the world.

7. Rocks of hope 

You will need: stones to paint; paint; brushes; a covering for your table or grass area

Use a stone to paint a picture of hope. It could be a rainbow, a smiley face, the word 'hope' or anything else that gives the image of hope.

Talk about what gives people hope.

I wonder... how can you show the hope of Jesus to your neighbourhood?

8. Light up your street

You will need: bin bags; rubbish grabbers; plastic gloves; rocks of hope from the previous activity

This is a street-cleaning operation with a difference. Not only will you be cleaning the streets with your Messy Church family, but you'll also be hiding words of hope by leaving your painted rocks of hope around the area.

Talk about why we are doing this – to be salt and light in our neighbourhood. People will see a clean street and find words of hope that will encourage and lift them.

I wonder… what makes you hopeful?

9. Where in the world?

You will need: a large map of the world (this can be hand drawn on a large roll of paper); Post-it notes; pens; printed out news stories of injustices happening around the world at the moment (e.g. wars, refugees, poverty, slavery)

Pile the news stories up into one area of the map. The Messy Church family needs to read the story and put it into the place where they think the story is from. Use the Post-it notes to encourage people to write their own prayers for that country and place them on the map.

Talk about why there is so much injustice in the world. What makes you sad?

I wonder… will injustice ever disappear from the world?

10. God's big family

You will need: access to the internet; Open Doors UK have a World Watch List which looks at some of the hardest places to be a Christian in the world and they have some resources for children and families that you can look at (opendoorsuk.org/gods-big-family); A4 paper; pens; scissors

For older children, you could talk about the World Watch List. For younger children, you could make a people chain. Cut a piece of A4 paper in half lengthwise. Fold it in four. Draw a picture of a person ensuring that the hands and feet reach the ends of the page. Cut it out. Unfold. You now have four people holding hands. Decorate each person. There are videos on the Open Doors website that you could have playing, if possible.

Talk about about how we are all part of God's big family across the world. Use the people chain to represent this.

I wonder… how can you connect with God's big family across the world?

Celebration

The celebration is based on the Bible passage found in Matthew 5:13–16.

You will need: someone dressed up as a saltshaker (this could be as simple as getting someone to hold a bottle of salt or as complicated as creating a cardboard cut-out of a saltshaker for them to wear); someone dressed up as a light (again, this can be as simple or as complicated as desired); someone as a 'bouncer'; a bowl; mobile phone lights or torches; battery-powered tealights.

Read the Bible passage as summarised below. As you are reading, the salt and light people should be moving as directed by the passage.

You are the salt of the earth. *The salt comes up on to the stage near the storyteller.*

But if the salt loses it saltiness, how can it be made salty again? *The storyteller and the salt try to taste the salt – lick finger – it tastes of nothing. Both pull a face.*

It is no longer good for anything, except to be thrown out and trampled underfoot. *Get a 'bouncer' to come and usher the salt off the stage.*

You are the light of the world. *The light comes up on to the stage near the storyteller.*

A town built on a hill cannot be hidden.

Neither do people light a lamp and put it under a bowl. *The 'bouncer' tries to put a bowl on the lights head.*

Instead, they put it on its stand, and it gives light to everyone in the house. *The light twirls around and gives battery tealights to everyone.*

In the same way, let your light shine before others, that they may see your good deeds and glorify your Father in heaven.

You see, we are called to be SALT and LIGHT in the world. To be light in the dark places that we face. To be salt and help more people to know who Jesus is.

I wonder...

- How can we be salt and light in our communities?
- What was your favourite part of the story and why?

Prayer

Ask everyone to lift their candles up as you say a prayer.

Lord, thank you that you have called us to be hope in your world. Help us to be salt and light to those we meet this week. Amen.

Song suggestions

- 'City on a hill' – Nick and Becky Drake (Worship for Everyone)
- 'Let your light shine' – Hillsong Kids
- 'This little light of mine' – Go Fish
- 'Shine (from the inside out)' – Spring Harvest
- 'We are one' – Mark and Helen Johnson (Out of the Ark Music)
- 'Take care of the world' – iSingPOP

Meal suggestions

Fish fingers and chips (with the option of adding salt), followed by jelly and ice cream.

Session material: August
Patience: wait for it!
By Anne Offler and Sharon Pritchard

Bible story for prep

Genesis 8:1–19 (MSG)

Then God turned his attention to Noah and all the wild animals and farm animals with him on the ship. God caused the wind to blow and the floodwaters began to go down. The underground springs were shut off, the windows of Heaven closed and the rain quit. Inch by inch the water lowered. After 150 days the worst was over.

On the seventeenth day of the seventh month, the ship landed on the Ararat mountain range. The water kept going down until the tenth month. On the first day of the tenth month the tops of the mountains came into view. After forty days Noah opened the window that he had built into the ship.

He sent out a raven; it flew back and forth waiting for the floodwaters to dry up. Then he sent a dove to check on the flood conditions, but it couldn't even find a place to perch – water still covered the Earth. Noah reached out and caught it, brought it back into the ship.

He waited seven more days and sent out the dove again. It came back in the evening with a freshly picked olive leaf in its beak. Noah knew that the flood was about finished.

He waited another seven days and sent the dove out a third time. This time it didn't come back.

In the six-hundred-first year of Noah's life, on the first day of the first month, the flood had dried up. Noah opened the hatch of the ship and saw dry ground. By the twenty-seventh day of the second month, the Earth was completely dry.

God spoke to Noah: 'Leave the ship, you and your wife and your sons and your sons' wives. And take all the animals with you, the whole menagerie of birds and mammals and crawling creatures, all that swarming extravagance of life, so they can reproduce and flourish on the Earth.'

Noah disembarked with his sons and wife and his sons' wives. Then all the animals, crawling creatures, birds – every creature on the face of the Earth – left the ship family by family.

Pointers

- Noah waited, and waited, and waited some more. He had already waited 150 days for the rain to stop. When it did, he still had to wait. What he wanted – to get off the ark – was not possible straight away. The earth had to dry out to enable him, his family and all the animals to live on it.

- Noah sent out a raven and then a dove. Both confirmed there was still more waiting to be done – another seven days!

- Finally, the dove came back with the branch which was the sign that all was ready. But still Noah had had to be patient, because he did not know how long it would be before they could leave the ark. Even when the rain stopped, he had to be patient while the earth dried out.

- We have to wait for many things today – a special event, a date or time to be reached, things to be ready. Just like Noah, often there are things we cannot hurry. We just have to be patient and wait.

- Are we calmly patient or is our waiting done in a state of agitation?

How does this session help people grow in Christ?

We hope to grow in patience as we see that in some situations we have to wait. We wait for events or for people to be able to understand or do something. We practise waiting calmly rather than in a state of agitation, and we think of others around us as we appreciate their waiting too.

Add value:

Mealtime card

- What kinds of things are you good at waiting for?
- What is the longest time you have had to wait for?

- Who do you know who is patient?
- How do we show patience to others?

Question to start and end the session

So… can we be more patient in our waiting if we practise?

Social action idea

Choose one of the prayer pointers in activity 10 to remember in your prayers until your next Messy Church. Maybe there is something you can do to help others who are waiting.

Activities

2. Build an ark  

You will need: the template of an ark PDF; small craft boxes; coloured pens or paint pens; animal stickers or pictures; PVA glue; double-sided tape

Use the template and fold the ark. Use the double-sided tape to stick the box in the bottom and to join the sides of the ark. Decorate the ark using pens or paints – wait for it to dry. (You could sing one of the Noah's ark songs, e.g. 'Mr Noah built an ark' or 'The animals came in two-by-two hurrah, hurrah!') Stick on some animals.

Talk about what it would have been like on the ark. How would it have been at first? What about later on? What about when they were waiting for the dove to come back? Are you good at waiting?

I wonder… is it easy to wait with other people? How can we help others to wait patiently?

3. Origami dove  

You will need: sheets of paper (origami or copier) eight inches square; the instruction sheet PDF; a small hole punch; thread

Make up the doves according to the instructions. Punch a small hole at the top of the back between the wings. Use thread to make a loop to hang up your dove.

Talk about the dove in the story. What was its special job? The dove today is a sign of peace. Do we need to develop patience to develop peace?

I wonder… if we were patient with one another, would we find peace?

1. Two by two 

You will need: playing cards with animals on them (two cards each with the same animal); a box

This works well in a large group and in a defined space. Ask each player to choose a card and, without anyone else seeing the animal on it, begin to walk around the space making the sound the animal makes. The spare cards can be on a table. When you find someone making the same animal sound compare cards, put your cards in the box and pick up another card from the table. Make the new sound and find a new partner.

Talk about how easy or difficult it was to recognise your animal partner only using the sounds they made? Did you have to keep trying? What helped you to keep going?

I wonder… what else do we have to keep trying until we manage to do it?

4. Practising patience! 

You will need: copies of the patience PDF for each person; pens or pencils; Bibles

Work your way through the patience puzzle sheet, using a Bible to look up the passage.

Talk about how patience isn't easy! How can we work together to make it easier?

I wonder… how can we show patience today?

5. Churn it over 

You will need: clean jars with fitting lids; double cream; bowls; a knife; bread and/or crackers; the instructions PDF

Remember to risk assess for allergies and intolerances.

Fill the jar one quarter full of cream. Put the lid on it tightly. Holding the top and bottom of the jar, shake the jar. Keep shaking until you can see a blob of butter. It will have watery liquid in the jar with it. Pour off the watery liquid and put the blob of butter on to a plate. Take a piece of bread or cracker and try some of your own freshly made butter, allergies permitting.

Talk about how long it took to make butter. Did you feel like giving up? Sometimes it's hard to be patient and to wait. How can we get better at being patient?

I wonder… what makes waiting easier?

6. Suck it and see!

You will need: fruit pastilles or chocolate buttons for younger participants; sand timers for 30 seconds, 1 minute, 5 minutes; a comfy sitting area

Remember to risk assess for allergies and intolerances.

Make yourself comfortable. Take a pastille or a chocolate button and pop it into your mouth. Turn the timers to start them and challenge the participants not to chew the pastille or chocolate button. Can they last 30 seconds? 1 minute? 5 minutes? Chew any of the remaining sweet. Who are the champions?

Talk about how you did. Did it get harder to resist the urge to chew? Did you keep watching the timer hoping it would go faster? Do you think time goes slowly when you are waiting for something?

I wonder… does staying calm and quiet helps you listen to God?

7. Chalk it up  

You will need: washable chunky pavement/ sidewalk chalks; the pictures of traditional olive branches PDF

Use the giant chalks to draw huge olive branches in your outdoor space. You may prefer to use large sheets of cardboard to cover the ground, especially if this is to be done indoors.

Talk about how the dove came back to Noah the second time with an olive branch showing that the earth was ready for the people and animals to leave the ark. The waiting was over and the next phase was about to begin. How can we make our church ready to welcome others and take the next steps in our growth?

I wonder… sometimes does the work begin when the waiting is over? What's your experience?

8. Hunt it out 

You will need: the hunt it out PDF; double-sided sticky tape; pencils and crayons; a clipboard with sheet of paper/card attached (optional)

Look at the colours of the things in the Noah story. Can you look around and find something that matches some of the colours? If it is safe to do so and not damaging to flowers, plants or the environment, pick up a small sample of the colour and stick it on the tape beside the colour. If you prefer, draw or write the name of the item instead.

Talk about Noah and the people on the ark. How do you think they had to be patient? Do you think it was easy?

I wonder… can we practise being patient when things seem a bit messy?

9. Olive branch prayers 

You will need: twigs or wire for branches; green crepe paper; florist tape; gift tags; pens or pencils

Cut out olive leaves from the crepe paper and attach them to the branches. Once you have an olive branch, write your prayer, asking God to help you be patient, on to a gift tag or tags and attach them to the branch.

Talk about how we can ask God to help us with anything we find difficult, especially when we need to be patient.

I wonder… what prayers did Noah and the others pray on the ark? What's your prayer?

10. Time to wait and pray 

You will need: paper plates; split pins; pencils; coloured pens; card; scissors

Make a clock, segmenting it into things that we are waiting to see happen locally and in the wider world, e.g. for wars to end, for peace, or to use the world's resources better. With the card, make two pointers and attach them to the clock with a split pin.

Talk about the things you have drawn as you turn the hands on your clock. Say a prayer together for this part of your clock.

I wonder… how long do things take to change and what can I do?

Celebration

How long is a minute? Let's see…

Ask for as many people who want to try to guess how long a minute is to stand up or raise their hand.

Without looking at watches, phones or anything else, sit down or put down your hand when you think a minute has passed starting now. *Look at your watch and note who sits closest to one minute and then announce the winner.*

Sometimes we have to wait lots of minutes before we can do something or go somewhere or get something we are waiting for.

How many minutes do you think there are until we get our Messy food? *Work it out, e.g. 19 minutes.*

How many minutes until our next Messy Church? *4 weeks = 40,320 minutes.*

How many minutes until my birthday? (Well that's a long way off, so there are lots and lots.)

How many minutes did Noah wait after the dove came back with the branch in its beak? He waited 10,080. So how do you think he waited? Do you think he paced up and down. *Invite people to pace up and down.*

Do you think he stomped around? *Invite people to stomp around.*

Do you think he sat and got more and more impatient? *Sit and show increasing impatience, e.g. looking at clock, shaking head, sighing.*

Do you think he decided to wait calmly and patiently, just getting on with what he was doing? *Invite people to smile and say, 'Not long now.'*

If he had to wait for 10,080 minutes, do you think pacing up and down or stomping or being angry and impatient or waiting calmly made the time go faster? The time didn't change no matter what Noah did. Noah knew that soon the waiting would be over.

I wonder how we wait for things to happen. Sometimes I think we do get angry, frustrated, impatient. *Invite an appropriate action for each of these.* Sometimes when we wait calmly and patiently, even if we are excited, we feel better and enjoy what we are waiting for just a little more. Maybe people around us are a little happier when we are patient too.

Let's have a challenge to think about Noah waiting and waiting and waiting and see when we have to wait, whether we can do this calmly and even with a little smile.

I wonder...

- Have you been patient with someone recently?
- Are you a patient waiter?
- What/who can help us grow more patient?

Prayer

Ask people to do some gestures and expressions show-ing they are impatient and tired of waiting. Begin the prayer, noting the actions in italics, which might need to be practised.

Loving Lord,
Help us to be patient in our waiting. *Become calm, change facial expressions.*
Patient in our doing and trying. *Mime with hands some-thing we would like to do.*
Patient with our family and friends. *Look up and smile at people around us.*
Patient with ourselves. *Give ourselves a hug.*
Help us to grow in patience. *Bend down and slowly stand as if growing taller.*
Thank you that you are patient with us. *Touch fingers to lips and away as in sign language.*
Amen. *Hold hands together as praying hands.*

Song suggestions

- 'Arky arky (Rise and shine)' – Listener Kids
- 'Living and learning' – Mark and Helen Johnson (Out of the Ark Music)
- 'Patience' – Nick and Becky Drake (Worship for Everyone)

Meal suggestions

Pizza. Cook simple Margherita pizzas and have a selection of toppings for people to add. Ensure that all toppings are cooked through. Examples include ham, sweetcorn, tuna, grated cheese, bacon, peppers, mushrooms and onions.